MANIFESTING WITH THE

ANGELS

ALSO BY CHARLES VIRTUE
(WITH DOREEN VIRTUE)

BOOKS

Signs from Above
Awaken Your Indigo Power

CARD DECK

Indigo Angel Oracle Cards

All of the above are available online and
at your local bookstore. Please visit:

Charles's website: www.CharlesVirtue.com
Hay House USA: www.hayhouse.com®
Hay House Australia: www.hayhouse.com.au
Hay House UK: www.hayhouse.co.uk
Hay House India: www.hayhouse.co.in

MANIFESTING WITH THE ANGELS

ATTRACT A LIFE OF HAPPINESS,

PURPOSE, AND FULFILLMENT

WITH HEAVEN'S HELP

CHARLES VIRTUE

HAY HOUSE, INC.
Carlsbad, California • New York City
London • Sydney • New Delhi

Published in the United States by: Hay House, Inc.: www.hayhouse.com®
• **Published in Australia by:** Hay House Australia Pty. Ltd.: www.hayhouse.
com.au • **Published in the United Kingdom by:** Hay House UK, Ltd.: www.
hayhouse.co.uk • **Published in India by:** Hay House Publishers India: www.
hayhouse.co.in

Cover design: Barbara LeVan Fisher
Interior design: Pamela Homan

Library of Congress Cataloging-in-Publication Data

Names: Virtue, Charles, author.
Title: Manifesting with the angels : attract a life of happiness, purpose,
    and fulfillment with heaven's help / Charles Virtue.
Description: 1st edition. | Carlsbad : Hay House, Inc., 2018.
Identifiers: LCCN 2017052988 | ISBN 9781401951177 (tradepaper : alk.
paper)
Subjects: LCSH: Spiritual life. | Spirituality. | Archangels. | Angels.
Classification: LCC BL624 .V58 2018 | DDC 202/.15--dc23 LC record available
at https://lccn.loc.gov/2017052988

ISBN: 978-1-4019-5117-7

1st edition, January 2018

Printed in the United States of America

This book is dedicated to heaven,
the angels, the universe, and my lovely
wife, Peroshini Naidoo—without all
of these amazing forces in my life, this
book would not have been possible.

CONTENTS

Preface: The Missing Manifestation Ingredient ix

PART I: Tools and Principles of Manifestation

INTRODUCTION: Manifesting My Life Purpose 3

CHAPTER 1: Manifesting Happiness through Purpose. . . . 17
CHAPTER 2: Visualization and Affirmations. 33
CHAPTER 3: Asking for Help from Heaven 49
CHAPTER 4: Answered Prayers. 65
CHAPTER 5: Divine Timing 79

PART II: Clearing Blocks and Attracting Happiness,
Purpose, and Fulfillment with the Angels

CHAPTER 6: Harnessing the Power of Your Inner
Passion with Archangel Nathaniel. 97
CHAPTER 7: Dispelling Fears with Archangel Michael. . . 115
CHAPTER 8: Clearing the Often Unseen:
Karma and Cords 127
CHAPTER 9: Healing from Past Pain
with Archangel Raphael 147

Afterword: Spreading Joy 163
Appendix:
   • *Archangels of Manifestation* 173
   • *Manifestation Prayers*. 179
About the Author 191

PREFACE

The Missing Manifestation Ingredient

A lot of manifestation teachings already exist, I know, but through all of the books, movies, and seminars that I have been exposed to, I could never shake the feeling that something fundamental was missing. I am not here to criticize anyone else; I respect everyone who works hard to improve the world by teaching us how to master our thoughts. However, while the topic of manifestation has been covered many times, the simple fact is that not a single book covers the topic completely.

If you think about it, if any of them worked unfailingly, no one (including yourself) would feel the need to take in any more information on the subject. Please don't think that I am in any way saying other manifestation books are not effective. No doubt they are—each in its own way. What I am saying is that manifestation is a very complex topic and from my observations, many books get a few points right but omit some essential aspects related to healing, self-reflection, and energetic blocks, a lapse that always left me wanting more.

What's missing isn't some manifestation "magic." Our power to attract the life of our dreams isn't something that can be turned on or off—it has always been within us. However, to get in touch with our higher selves—the aspect of us that knows no fear and has no ego, and knows what is best for us—there are some important steps to take and blocks to clear.

MY PURPOSE AS A TEACHER

For the last decade of my life, I have been traveling around the world to over 25 countries teaching the art of manifesting with the angels. In this time, I have seen so many amazing transformations that have only further fueled my drive to teach more. When people realize that heaven, God, and the angels are on their side—that they want to help, and accessing that help is something each of us can do—a lot of smiles appear, but a lot of questions arise as well.

Growing up, my mother would always tell me, "The angels will bring you whatever you want; you just have to ask." As nice as this was to hear, I also found it difficult to believe. I would think, *If I can have anything I want, why* don't *I?*

The answer the angels would give me always confused me: "Charles, you *do* have exactly what you want—what you 'want' is what you put your energy into, not just what you ask for."

That was a real eye-opener for me—and over the years, as I worked to clear my blocks of fear and doubt, I noticed a divine truth to the angels' words.

Every single one of us has a divine ability to create and attract literally whatever we want. This simple fact is repeated many different ways in everything taught about the law of attraction, the basis of manifestation. The law of attraction states that thoughts and emotions are like a magnet, the polarization of which is based exclusively on the energy we put into them. It is undeniable how much power we have to turn our thoughts into reality, and it is not a force or phenomenon that is determined by our faith, diet, confidence level, or heritage—it is something all humans can do, and it cannot be turned off.

So naturally you may be wondering, *If it is so easy, then why isn't everyone wealthy, happy, and living the life of their dreams?*

It's a good question, and I challenge you to consider this—everyone *is* living the life of their dreams: the life their thoughts and energy created. The problem is, we are spending too much time dreaming and thinking about what does not serve us.

If you are confused or upset by reading this, it would be a normal and quite understandable reaction, especially if you are one of the many, many people on this planet who feel life could definitely be better. It can be frustrating to hear that certain patterns and issues you face may be as a result of your own thought process. This is part of the reason why so many people are stuck in repetitive life patterns, though—it can be frightening to reassess your thinking and priorities. It can be even more frightening to actually do something about it.

WHAT IS MANIFESTATION?

Manifestation is an all-encompassing force that takes into consideration the sum of your thoughts, your imagination, your reaction to your surroundings, and your personal sense of eligibility for happiness. Our culture also plays a big role in what and how we manifest—and, dare I say, a lot of what we are exposed to in life works wonders to help us deploy our power against ourselves.

Just because we have the ability and power to turn our thoughts into reality does not mean we always know how to do it in a beneficial way. When we spend too much time allowing ourselves to be exposed to fearful things—like the news, in most cases—it subconsciously programs us to believe in and focus on a world full of fear and suffering. When we live our lives thinking that these sorts of tragic situations are normal and "just life," we literally use our thoughts to help create that reality. If you think about it objectively, our world can be peaceful any moment we collectively decide it should be. It's 100 percent up to us!

So when it comes time to pray, or put physical effort into improving our lives in any way, we tend to think on a more limited scale—the fear the outside world sometimes inundates us with has the unfortunate consequence of teaching us to make "safe" and "calculated" decisions based solely on our own projection of our ability and eligibility to attract these improvements. When we have lived a life full of disappointment and letdown, it can be very easy to assume, if even subconsciously, that this is par for the course—and we limit our desires accordingly to align with the "reality" we have come to know.

Join me for a little journey . . .

Simply put, we always attract whatever we want—without exception. You do this, I do this, everyone does this—it's how the energy of existence works. And the more you work toward improving your life, the more you will realize that you were not a victim of circumstance as much as you might have once thought—you were, in fact, a product of your thoughts.

The guilt, doubt, and hesitation regarding happiness that our society programs into our psyche are the first, and by far the most important, hurdles to cross when manifesting with the angels. If you have doubt, even in the deepest parts of your mind, you dilute and needlessly delay happiness. Why do that?

It is said that God loves us unconditionally. It is also said that God gave us complete free will. I believe these both to be irrefutable facts. Free will states that we, as a species, are allowed to create whatever world we desire—we are given everything we need to survive—and what we do with our time and the resources on this planet is completely up to us. The rules of the universe dictate that *like* attracts *like* . . . and all energy will take the path of least resistance.

That explains gravity and electricity—but it also explains the conundrum of human existence.

The first thing we must understand about God and the universe is their neutrality. You see, God loves us and wants the best for us, but it is up to us to find the best for ourselves. At no point should we ever hold God responsible for the bad things that happen in our world: God didn't draw borders; we did. God didn't say one group of humans should have more power or control than others; the human ego, the fear-based, limited aspect of ourselves that often tricks itself into believing that we are not worthy and others can be greater than us, did.

If you think about it—and with all due respect— the world we live in, and the state of affairs as they currently exist, is all a result of mainstream, fear-based thinking. The world you see around you is the culmination of millennia of the same type of mind-set, and while the world has many, many great things we should all appreciate, it is beyond debate that there are many, many improvements that must be made.

A lot of people claim to *not* know the meaning of life—but if you look around, the meaning is pretty clear: to rid ourselves of fear on a planetwide scale. The biggest and most consistent issue on this planet is fear. It is the root of all of the terrible things we have done to each other—throughout history. Fear is what tells us that in order to be happy we must take what we think we want and need from others. Not coincidentally, lifting the blocks of fear and eradicating the mind-set of scarcity are also the keys to successful manifestation.

The belief that your happiness is contingent on the actions of others is the greatest flaw in the human mentality. This thought process is what was at the root of literally every war or major human conflict. "You have what I want—and in order for me to find happiness within myself, I must take it from you" is the underlying mission statement of all of our worst deeds in recorded history.

This belief that the ingredients for happiness are available in a limited quantity—and we must do whatever it takes to get our share before someone else takes it—is a very, very prominent mentality that spans cultures, governments, corporations, and religions.

The fact is that the backbone of capitalism is fleeting happiness and temporary highs. We are programmed from a young age to constantly chase that next thrill and are often compelled to achieve success for the material gains it will afford us. Sadly, in a lot of ways, material goods have replaced God in our world. Our motivation is sometimes based more on "What's in it for me?" than "How can I make the world a better place?"

But what if I told you that we could let go of this fear—that this illusion of limitation we created and perpetuated was completely baseless and false? What if I told you that literally everything you will ever need to find true happiness and your unique divine purpose is out there in the world waiting for you, and when you need it—when you *really* need it (not just when your fear tells you it's needed)—it will be there for you at no loss to anyone else on this planet?

That is God's truth. We are allowed to live happy lives, and everything we need to do so is here waiting for us. God wants us to know that the dog-eat-dog age of survival is behind us, and we are now awakening into a new, enlightened era where limitless possibilities for purpose and peace are all around us.

It is time for us to take control of our thoughts, and, therefore, our lives, and decide definitively that we individually and collectively can choose happiness on this planet. Of course, this can seem like an overwhelming task, but heaven is on our side. Although God and the angels will not live our lives for us, this doesn't mean they are not right there to help us in any way we may need them.

God wants you to be happy as much as *you* want to be happy—and the angels are here to bring God's love and guidance into every aspect of your life, if you ask for and allow it.

BELIEVE IT AND YOU'LL ACHIEVE IT!

It's very easy for our minds to become overwhelmed and distracted when we start to contemplate the seemingly daunting magnitude of changing our lives from how they are today to what we picture in our dreams . . . and heaven understands. The good news is that we are almost never meant to take on the totality of all that change at once. It wouldn't serve us, and in most situations it certainly would not further our life purpose.

Why do you think all of the gurus of manifestation, like Wayne Dyer and Tony Robbins, say over and over, "Believe it and you'll achieve it!"? It's because of the simple fact that most people refuse to *believe* they are capable of doing something great without some sort of proof. Most are convinced that there has to be something different about themselves—something inherently gifted—in order for them to achieve true happiness in life.

Isn't it interesting how happy and successful people talk so much about how important it is to align your thoughts with your desires—and those who feel life is working *against* them will tell you that the world isn't fair and suffering is an inevitability?

When you listen to successful people talking about how they made it, you'll always hear them prefacing their stories with what first went on in their minds and hearts. Successful people live in a world where what we consider to be logical limitations, such as money, time, and ability, simply don't exist! The successful people I am talking about are the ones who started off with nothing (and there are more of them than you might realize). Most people assume these individuals must have had some sort of advantage, because if it were really that easy to accomplish, surely they, too, would have thought of a way by now.

Too many of us don't realize that by placing seemingly logical conditions on our lives, we are basically telling the universe: "I don't want this."

- *I can't afford to do this. [So I don't want this.]*

- *I have a job and could never find the time. [So I don't want this.]*

- *How on earth would I succeed? [So I don't want this.]*

You get the picture. Whenever we place limitations on our dreams, however logical the limitations may seem, we are building a wall between them and us.

We have a tendency to plan tomorrow based only on the resources available to us today—not taking into consideration how much can (and always will) change as time goes on. One of my favorite sayings is "To get what you've never had, you've got to do what you've never done." I simply ask you to not shut down to the idea of happiness just because it may not seem easy or even possible to attain. The universe is listening, and if you seek fulfillment and purpose, you simply need to ask . . . and allow yourself to believe there is a chance all of this is true.

Another one of my favorite sayings is "Whether you think you can or you can't—you're right!" To find and maintain a happy life, you must first find and maintain the discipline to believe it's possible.

This is exactly why I wrote this book. Our relationship with manifestation often leaves us in limbo, with the hope and motivation we feel for the future dueling with the frustration and fear we feel when actually processing the idea of taking forward action.

Manifestation can seem like a very lonely endeavor, but it doesn't have to feel this way. We aren't alone in this world, and we need to stop acting like we are. God and the angels not only want us to find happiness—they actually *insist* we do, because the journey to and discovery of joy, peace, and balance on our planet is the very point of our existence.

All I ask of you as you read this book is to remain open to a new way of thinking and processing the world around you. I do not want to conflict with your beliefs or impose new beliefs upon you—but after working with thousands of people all over the planet, I can assure you that happiness is a real possibility and attainable by all.

PART I

TOOLS AND PRINCIPLES OF MANIFESTATION

INTRODUCTION

Manifesting My Life Purpose

Since I was a child, my mother has reminded me to watch my thoughts. She said that aligning them with positive energy, like the angels, has beneficial effects, while even joking about or processing negative or violent energy could and would negatively affect my life.

I used to get really frustrated hearing this because it felt like I had no freedom to have fun, or just be a typical little boy. I liked cartoons, video games, and toys that sometimes portrayed violence—a lot of little boys (and girls!) do. It didn't feel harmful while I was being exposed to them, but now that I am an adult, I realize that damage *was* actually being done.

My mother, Doreen Virtue, has been working with angels for the last 25-plus years and really knows what she's talking about. When my brother and I were born, my parents were very young and not financially solvent—therefore, we relied on family and government assistance to survive. Growing up around my mother was fascinating because even though we had next to nothing—above and beyond what we needed to stay alive—she always imagined her life completely differently from what most would have considered to be the "reality" of our existence.

The truth of our world is that there are no limits. And watching my mother go from a teenage mother to a successful author, speaker, and teacher has shown me so beyond a doubt. If we are willing to muster the discipline to keep our thoughts laser-focused on our dreams and put in the work to constantly analyze ourselves and work to improve not only our thought patterns but our energetic connections (which I explain in depth later in this book), there is *nothing* we cannot achieve. If that sounds unbelievable to you, I'm very happy we get to spend this time together so I can show you what I hope you will consider to be a new way of living your life.

OUR PROGRAMMING

From a young age, I was programmed through games and television to accept that there are definitive "good guys" and "bad guys." It became natural to believe that there were forces in the world that were simply out to get us. For a lot of people, those principles solidify to form the basis of a good portion of the divisiveness we know in the world today.

Another disturbing life dynamic that flashed in front of me on the screen is that life isn't fair, and there is one set formula for success and happiness: Go to school, get a job, and don't make any trouble for the world around you. It was commonplace to see the plot of a TV show centering on someone who thought the rules didn't apply to them. They would try an alternative route to success, only to find in the end that conformity and careful planning were the only true keys to life—and everyone is better off just following that path.

These shows basically vilified alternative thinking, such as believing you really can achieve greatness, and promoted conformity as the surest way to live your life. The irony of these terrible lessons is that the actors who portrayed the characters in these situations were themselves living examples of pursuing and achieving great life goals.

So it's no surprise today that in so many social circles people often find themselves too ashamed or self-conscious to ever talk about big dreams or aspirations that seem statistically improbable. Most people would discount large ambitions as pipe dreams or fantasies.

Throughout my years of teaching and in countless personal angel readings I have given, I have spoken to so many people around the world who feel as if they live a double life because they have to divide their time between dreaming of the life they want and actually living the one that they've ended up with. So they wait and wait for change to come, and some have almost given up on happiness because things never seem to change for the better.

So why is it that with all this power to attract whatever we want, situations like the one I just described are so commonplace, so much so that I'm sure anyone reading this book can relate on some level? What is it about our world, our thoughts, and our way of life that keeps us from living lives full of purpose and fulfillment? Are we doing something wrong? Is there a step we missed somewhere along the way?

The answer to those questions and others like them comes with understanding exactly how energy flows, and how our thoughts work. As I discovered, these principles of manifestation are paradoxical in nature: both incomprehensibly complex and laughably simple.

THE PATH TO PURPOSE

When I first resolved to start teaching about angels and manifestation, ready to decide that fear was less important than my life purpose, my mother was elated. She instantly opened her laptop and said, "I'm going to help you get started!" I was thrilled and terrified all at the same time as I watched her type an e-mail to about 10 event producers she regularly worked with around the world. The e-mail said something like this: "Hello, everyone: it's Doreen! I am so excited to let you know that my son Charles is finally ready to answer his calling and teach angel classes in cities and countries I can no longer travel to. I would be so honored if you would consider inviting Charles to your city." She hit *send*, and we said a small prayer together.

Over the next week or two, replies to the e-mail started coming in—and my mother was always so excited that she would call me and say, "We got another reply!" As she read them to me, I can't say I was totally surprised when they all contained a message like this: "Hello, Doreen: It's so great to hear from you! We are excited to hear your son is going to start teaching; you must be so proud. We aren't ready to invite him to our country yet, but if *you* ever plan to come back, please let us know."

E-mail after e-mail all said pretty much the same thing. I will be honest: there was a moment when I thought, *Well, the people have spoken; my fears were right. Maybe I'm not meant to be an angel teacher.* That moment was, fortunately, very brief because I knew deep in my heart that I was meant to help bring positive change to this world—I just didn't know how. So I kept praying and just let the matter go to the best of my ability. Eventually, one of the last e-mail replies to come back was from a company from Germany my mother worked with a lot. The owner was actually interested in discussing the possibility of having me teach in Hamburg!

So at this point I had nine *no*'s and one *maybe*—hardly the statistic our logical minds would say is the basis of a career, but I was excited beyond belief.

I have a lot of friends in Germany and I was coincidentally (or divinely) scheduled to be in Berlin around the time the company owner wanted to meet, so I made a lunch appointment. When we met, I was so nervous—I had no idea what to say. How do you plan a class when you've literally never taught one before? Luckily he was a professional and asked me great questions about format, length, and pricing (yikes!).

When the meeting was over, he said he would get back to me in a week or so with a firm answer. So I took a train back to Prenzlauer Berg (a section of east Berlin) and waited to hear back. Even though on paper the odds of my being able to turn my life into the one I was dreaming of were slim, I still kept the faith, prayed every day, and tried my best to surrender the situation to heaven.

Needless to say, the universe being what it is, the answer I ultimately received from Hamburg was a positive one, and I was now scheduled to teach my first class.

ANSWERING THE CALL

What I don't talk about as often as the story I just told is the time right before I made the decision to start teaching. When I was younger, I always knew I wanted to help people, but I never, ever saw myself in front of a crowd. You see, I always suffered from severe shyness, and when I say *severe*, that is no exaggeration. Whenever my mother would make a spectacle of me in front of her classes (which I was always recruited to help with), my face would instantly turn red, my lips would quiver, and sometimes I could even feel my own pounding pulse in my face—it was bad.

I just wasn't a public-type person and felt infinitely more comfortable in intimate settings with maybe three or four people, certainly not hundreds. So every time my mother would tell me (and this was often), "Charles, someday you're going to take over when I retire and teach angel classes in front of a crowd," I honestly thought she didn't know me at all. How in the world could someone as shy as I was possibly teach a class when I struggled to complete a sentence in front of more than a few strangers?

So when I thought about my future and what I wanted to do with my life, the seemingly logical choice for me was the medical field. I wanted to be a doctor, and when I started college, I took classes in accordance with that plan. It made perfect sense to me. Once I became a doctor I would open a small general practitioner's office and live my life according to my shyness by seeing patients one-on-one in a small room that couldn't possibly hold more than three or four people. Perfect.

I decided that one great way to get hands-on medical experience would be to become certified as an emergency medical technician and work in an ambulance. I did just that—I became certified and started my internship. During school I felt so sure about my path, and it had felt so right that I had invested several years at this point in my premed education. So I was confused when during my internship, I felt zero connection to the work whatsoever. I really didn't feel the passion I felt while I was learning in the classroom, and this wasn't laziness—something about this work didn't speak to my soul.

I have always been very responsive to my gut feelings, so I instantly stopped my internship and dropped out of college altogether to reassess my life. *What now?* You can always tell if your gut feeling has something real and important to tell you if it doesn't change over time—if the feeling you're getting is consistent, you can trust it's a message to follow.

I still knew I had a purpose to help people, but I hadn't become less shy, so what could I possibly do? As luck would have it, my mother's company had an opening to help with event registrations, so I gladly took it. I worked for my mother for almost seven years when the inner guidance to answer my soul calling came back, louder than ever.

Just like when my guidance told me to stop pursuing a medical degree, I was now getting clear guidance to stop working for my mother. I knew this was because I was meant to do something more suited to my purpose, so I told my mother (she understood), and I quit working for her.

For the next two years, I sent literally hundreds of résumés out into the world, trying everything I could do to find a job that did not confront my fear of speaking in public. I was interviewed and hired at several companies—but each time I walked into work, I was instantly overwhelmed with the sensation that I did not belong there. So I kept quitting my jobs and kept looking for my purpose.

I will admit I am an extreme case when it comes to following my guidance—if the angels say it's time to move on, my bags are already packed. Change is exciting and thrilling to me—but I know I am in the minority for feeling that way.

A reasonable person might have stayed in at least one of those jobs just to pay the bills, and my mother was not supporting me financially at the time—she made it very clear when I quit that I was on my own. Yet I always somehow made just enough to survive; I had roommates, no vehicle, and minimal bills, so it was relatively easy.

When I look back, my life was actually perfectly designed for that transition period. It felt frightening while I was living it, and at times I felt very lost—but it really could not have gone any other way. The one aspect that never felt lost was my inner knowing that I was meant for something meaningful in life. I kept praying and asking heaven: "What am I supposed to do?" I always got the same answer: I was supposed to teach.

So after two years of trying to avoid my purpose, and with great trepidation, I eventually gave in and committed to being a teacher. I certainly do not do this work for money or fame. I would have made a very comfortable living as a doctor, of course, and I have never wanted to be famous, as I'm sure you can imagine. I do this work because I was born to do it—and the fears that kept me from accepting that were actually not a roadblock . . . they were a part of my path. If you feel similarly guided to follow your purpose, your fears may in fact be ensuring you lay the groundwork for manifesting the life of *your* dreams.

I have previously touched upon my manifestation experiences in books I co-wrote with my mother, *Signs from Above* and *Awaken Your Indigo Power*, but never before have I had the amazing opportunity to put everything I know about life purpose and manifestation into one book. Hopefully my story and what I've learned can inspire your own pursuit of the life of your dreams (whatever that means to you).

Over the years, my life and career have defied the odds because I refused to let fear and doubt take over. My teaching career almost didn't happen, but I kept my mind focused on wanting to help the world. Ten years later, I am still getting invitations to teach, and each one is incredibly appreciated. If it wasn't for the base knowledge of the angels my mother gave me—and the massive expansion of that knowledge I've acquired through my own personal relationship with the angels—I can assure you that my life would have turned out much, much differently.

As I will repeat throughout this book, nothing can bring the kind of lasting and sustainable inner peace that living a life of purpose can. My hope as you go through each chapter is that you'll see that while manifestation can seem complex and sometimes intimidating, it really is just about taking energetic responsibility for yourself—being aware of how you affect others and how your surroundings affect you.

Not only that, but guidance toward happiness has always been accessible to each of us—we just have to learn how to listen to heaven. In my 10 years of traveling and teaching, I have never met a person who could not connect to the angels—and I have never witnessed a moment when the angels have refused to work with a human.

Once you discover how you energetically inter-act with the world, you'll see beyond a doubt that there is a very clear path to follow—but you must first be open to the journey. Thank you for taking the first step with me in this book.

Blessings,
Charles

Chapter 1

MANIFESTING HAPPINESS THROUGH PURPOSE

Throughout my entire life I have spent what some may consider to be an excessive amount of time pondering the energetic dynamics and physical mechanics of our universe. I have logged thousands of hours studying the aspects of energy that seem to control the times when we can or cannot attract what makes us happy.

I always find it so interesting when I meet someone who seems to "have it all," and I study their actions and nuances closely. *It all* is such a subjective term, but in this instance, I mean happiness—people who appear to want for nothing and seem to operate under the assumption that life is a balanced, fair experience.

I am sure you've shared the same room with a few people like this in your life, and you know what I mean when I say that the energy they give off is almost captivating. A vicarious flow of their peace and tranquility seems to wash over you, and at the same time you find yourself comparing your life to theirs.

Some people at this point begin to bask in the light of such happy people and take this meeting as a divine portrayal of what they themselves wish to live like. Others may be watching these happy people closely, looking for holes in their stories, waiting for something that doesn't add up to appear and validate the suspicion that their lives are too good to be true. How we perceives these seemingly blessed few is very important to think about—because it's crucial to the discovery of our personal power of manifestation.

If you're the type of person who enjoys the company of happy people—if, after spending time around people who live lives that align with your dreams, *you* feel uplifted and happy—then I praise you for being a very evolved soul.

If you're like a lot of people on this planet, though, when you are in a situation where some-one has something you desire greatly, it brings you a pang of anxiety—a reminder of the absence in your life. Or, more notably, if you feel negatively toward those people because of jealousy, that does not mean you are "less than," less deserving, or less lucky. It simply means you have definitive blocks relating to achieving your dreams, and that's okay.

There's a divine place in this world for you. There are divine opportunities for you. There is a happy future you have access to, if you so choose.

The events in our past do not dictate a pattern for our future—it is only our minds, and our determination of our own reality, that allow patterns, good or bad, to be perpetuated. Just because things did not work before does not mean that all efforts in the future are doomed.

Everything can change, and for the better, in an instant. With heaven's help, suddenly our blocks can be lifted, and we find ourselves joining the ranks of those happy people who "have it all."

ARE *YOU* HAPPY?

The unending human quest for material comforts has led to some amazing innovations and conveniences for us all to enjoy, but do you think the people around you are *really* happy? Are they happy in a long-lasting, no-external-reason-required sort of way?

Are *you* happy? Is your life the one you imagined? Do you feel that you've reached your maximum potential, living in a way that aligns with your deepest desires?

Happiness is more than that fleeting feeling you get when something great happens, more than the temporary euphoria of meeting a compatible new love interest, more than the momentary joy of celebrating an accomplishment. True, divine, and pure happiness comes through an awareness that you were born for a reason—and that this reason aligns perfectly with your desires and inclinations.

Purpose does not mean an occupation; it does not relate to anything specific at all. It is simply what brings you lasting and sustainable happiness—which is what every human desires. And while we embody this happiness in different forms, the feeling of completion and fulfillment are what we are all, ultimately, after.

Just imagine for a moment waking up tomorrow and knowing exactly why you're alive, exactly why you are here—and on top of that, feeling complete fulfillment, knowing that your job and obligations for the day are exactly what you *want* to do, not just what you have to do. How does it feel to imagine that?

YOU ARE ALLOWED
TO LIVE A HAPPY LIFE

If you've never heard these words before, I am honored to be the first to tell you: *You are allowed to live a happy life.* Not only that, but your purpose on this earth *is* to be happy. Each and every one of us has a divine reason for being on this planet, and heaven, the angels, and God are so enthusiastic about working with us to discover why we are here and what happiness means to *us.*.

According to the law of God-given free will, we are allowed to live our lives however we want—we can choose to be happy and focus on spreading happiness, or we can choose to be more fearful. We are *so* free that it is often far too easy for people to give in to fear about the unknown—and maintain an overall pessimistic attitude about life. But there are no rules, universal or religious, stating that our world has to be chaotic and unpredictable.

Right now we live in a world that is predetermined only relative to the decisions humans have made up until this point. Nothing is set in stone or the product of a master plan—things simply are the way they are . . . because people have collectively decided on them. Life on this planet can change for the better, instantly, the moment we decide that it should.

Throughout this book, we are going to explore what manifestation is—*how* your thoughts, choices, and connections in life affect you in different ways—and ultimately, learn to open up to the divinity of following your angels' guidance. We are also going to work on examining *what* you are manifesting—your wants and desires—to determine if it is actually in your highest good. So much goes into the process of manifestation, and my goal for this book is to help you grasp the sometimes ambiguous-seeming principles, before we delve into our manifestation work with the angels (in Part II).

Manifesting with the angels is a process of working with the heavenly and loving beings that exist around and with each and every living soul on this planet to discover the sometimes mysterious and seemingly hidden path our lives are supposed to take. It is never too late, and you have always been qualified to have a happy life full of purpose.

WANTS AND DESIRES—
CONSCIOUS AND UNCONSCIOUS

Confusion arises because of the mass misunderstanding of what happiness actually means—and because we misdirect ourselves by thinking that we know what we actually want in life.

To clear up this confusion, we need to understand just exactly what the word *want* means, what it stands for. Most of us think of a *desire* or *want* in the context of our conscious minds, what it is we find ourselves regularly craving or needing . . . and that wouldn't be an inaccurate definition, but it would be an incomplete one.

Yes, wants are what we think about and what we desire, but we must understand that our conscious thoughts are only a fraction of who and what we are. Thoughts are the part of ourselves that we can control and interact with; thoughts are like the screen on a computer or smartphone. They give us updates on our opinions and allow us to analyze the world around us. However, our thoughts, like what we see on the screen, are merely feedback and an interface to inner workings that are infinitely more complex than most of us realize.

What you want is so much more than what you think about. Wants encompass all of the energy you express and allow yourself to hold on to each day. The entirety of who you are—thoughts, emotions, *everything*—is what you're telling the universe you want, and the universe always delivers.

Strictly speaking, a want is simply a solution, an answer to something missing or out of place. What we want is based on what we feel is lacking in our lives, or what we feel could be improved.

Our wants often live in categories in our minds, ranging from what we consider most attainable all the way to what we consider a fantasy—things that may or may not actually come to fruition, but we still *want* them. We are prone to making determinations in our minds as to which we can and cannot achieve and live our lives based on these often arbitrary limitations.

Our wants are multidimensional, however, and not always clear to us:

• Our **conscious wants** are often a product of what we have been exposed to in life, what we see others finding happiness in, and what marketing has routinely steered us toward, whether or not it is based in our own highest good. Simply put, a lot of us *want* things we don't *really* want.

Wants generally have a lot less to do with the actual desire than with its long-range outcome. When we want something, ultimately what we are after is the *experience* of receiving it and the *satisfaction* of having it. The emotions we feel when we obtain something we want are what we need to pay more attention to, because we all have a metaphorical or literal box somewhere, full of things we once "wanted" but no longer pay attention to.

Consider why luxury brands like Prada exist. They serve no purpose based in necessity—their products aren't without more practical and affordable alternatives. No one in the entire world *needs* Prada . . . but a lot of people *want* their products because those who are in possession of them are often seen as happier. When it comes to desires for material goods such as these, the item itself is not what we are after—we are actually chasing how we will feel (or how we think we will feel) once we have it.

• Our **unconscious wants** are the soul-based desires each of us has within us. These are the inner longings to do something *more* with our lives and feel the daily sense of fulfillment that comes with it. These desires are not always easy to pinpoint—I meet a lot of people in my classes and during my lectures who know they want happiness, but have no idea what that will eventually look like.

The more you understand your thoughts and those soul-based desires, the more aligned you'll become to what you really want, not just what you think you want. Not only that, but understanding fundamental principles about God and the universe, including manifestation, is the key to humanity's next evolution—it is the key to finding lasting happiness and peace on our planet. It's a worthwhile endeavor!

FALSE MANIFESTATIONS

Before we dive into our manifestation work, I want to point out a trap it's common to fall into. *False manifestations* are when we attract blocks to happiness through misdirected thoughts and energy, instead of listening to our hearts to find what would truly make us happy. I have identified several different types of false manifestations that we are all guilty of taking part in:

• **Comparing.** A lot of time negative feelings come because we compare ourselves to happy or successful people, thinking about how much work must have gone into them getting to where they are, and we become overwhelmed to the point of self-defeat just trying to imagine starting down a path of happiness for ourselves. This is especially true once we age into our thirties and beyond—we sometimes fall for the illusion that "it's too late now." But that could not be further from the truth.

Humans are a comparative species, and like it or not, all of us are guilty of looking at people around us and making determinations about their lives—and then deciding what aspects of those lives we would like to integrate into our own, so that we may experience the same level of happiness they seem to have. We often spend so much time fixating on what is popular or in demand that we constantly ignore our own guidance and we wonder why we can't ever seem to find lasting happiness.

• **Disallowing.** Another aspect of comparing yourself to other people is to think they are out of touch or to think, *Of course they can do that because they have the money*, which again is an example of separation thinking. Purpose is by no means synonymous with wealth or material abundance or anything like that, but you *will* always be taken care of if you allow it. I have actually worked with a lot of people who on a soul level were meant to be wealthier than they were, than they were *allowing* themselves to be deep down. Again, money is not the be-all and end-all. But just don't deny yourself something out of guilt or by supposing it to be so fantastical that it has to be unrealistic. If you're focusing on your lack, and envy is the way in which you're reacting to or expressing that, then you're going to manifest the results of that lower-energetic train of thought.

• **Working against yourself.** Believe it or not, you may actually be trapping yourself in a situation you don't like because you are putting so much energy into it that you are basically praying for it.

You see, free will is a gift *and* a responsibility. Heaven wants us to be happy . . . but the universe allows us to attract whatever we focus our thoughts and energy on. So if we decide to focus on our fears more than on our purpose, then those thoughts become our prayers—and prayers are always answered.

It's important to remember that there is a huge difference between manifesting toward something desirable, and manifesting "away" from something undesirable. The energy that you put into your manifestation should always be free of the past; instead, use the joy of knowing your prayers will be answered to fuel your continued faith and further prayer.

When you allow your mind and energy to exist in the reality you want more than in the life you are trying to escape, heaven and the universe see clearly that you want to move forward. When you spend so much time upset that you think more about what you want to get rid of or change in your life, heaven and the universe hear that as well.

I know it sounds strange, but the laws of manifestation often do not care if you are thinking *I don't want this* or *I really do want this* about a specific thing or situation. They just see that you are putting energy into it and are, therefore, attracting it.

If you are in a situation that you really want to get out of, please consider the way you are processing it energetically. I feel that it's almost better to sometimes live in a state of denial about what you don't like about your life if you find yourself obsessing over your problems. Whatever it takes to get the lower energy out of your mind, to replace that with the energy of exactly what you envision for your future, should always be your priority. In the past, I have taken up hobbies like playing video games just to keep my mind off my fears, doubts, and concerns, as I have found it to have almost meditative qualities because I can empty my mind and just enjoy being in the moment.

Traditionally, doing things like playing video games is seen as a waste of time—but no time is wasted when you're taking action to attune your energy to the vibration of your desires, and *only* your desires. Take a walk, go to the park or the movies, or binge on your favorite TV show. Although these are not usually considered to be productive activities, nothing in life is *less* productive than existing in fear of the unknown. It's okay to slack off in your free time if you feel it distracts you from working against yourself.

As you read this book and go through the manifestation exercises it contains, remember that even though you *will* do the actual work to find and live your unique divine purpose, heaven wants you to be relaxed and happy during the process. Many people think that the energy of laughter is very similar to the vibration of heaven, so go easy on yourself, because what you think about *matters*. The better your general attitude, the more your thoughts will work in your favor. The more you can energetically and emotionally separate yourself from a bad situation, the easier it is to cut ties to it and ensure it does not return.

The universe we live in allows us to use the power of our thoughts to create our reality. The universe doesn't care what we attract or why, but it is true that what we spend the most time thinking about is what we attract—good or bad. If we live in constant fear, we are often presented with good reason to continue doing so—and, thus, those who choose to live in fear are often confused as to why everyone else doesn't exercise the same level of vigilance and caution.

Conversely, those who live in peace and harmony find that life is full of love—and they, too, are confused as to how or why anyone would choose any other way to live.

When you allow yourself to freely dream of what you want in life, you connect with certain emotions. These emotions can tell you a lot about your current relationship with your purpose—and manifestation in general. If you dream of your desires, and find that you experience happiness and excitement, congratulations! Keep these emotions front and center because the more you allow yourself to feel the energy of your desires—the faster you attract them. Our interaction with the world around us consists mainly of our emotional response to it—so why not start letting yourself feel the joy of your dreams now?

CONNECTING WITH YOUR PURPOSE

We live in a complex world where we are inundated with so many stimuli that often our minds exist in a whirlwind of passing thoughts. We are encouraged to take on overwhelming schedules, and we barely have a few minutes a day between our obligations to think about anything else. Then, when we finally have a day or two off, we want to just unwind and do something fun and exciting—not think about life and our purpose for existing. This pattern often continues, virtually uninterrupted, until we reach an age when we simply decide that it is far too late to make any big changes.

Whether you can relate to this scenario or not, this is what's going on in the world around you—and this is a major contributor to the rampant unhappiness we see in this world.

Oftentimes, the mere idea of doing something different and more purposeful in life seems so impossibly complex as to keep us from spending too much time thinking about it. We instead think about money, our belongings, our reputation, and our relationships. Too many people allow their true purpose to hibernate in their subconscious, because the magnitude of the task of finding it can be frightening or it can even seem impossible to attain.

There is so much that goes into purpose—so much healing, growing, forgiving, and awakening—that charting a course to achieving it is an unfair burden to shoulder. So please consider being gentler on yourself, and instead of weighing yourself down with the "how," let yourself feel the joy of knowing it will come.

Chapter 2

VISUALIZATION AND AFFIRMATIONS

Have you ever wondered why it seems so easy for humans to attract unhappiness and pain? It's because we have zero doubt that those things can come true. We manifest them perfectly because our society lives under a spell that convinces us that there is a force out there working against our happiness. This, of course, could not be further from the truth, but we believe it and constantly create reasons to perpetuate the belief.

If you really think about it, on a universal scale, why would there be any difference between—let alone preference for—negative outcomes versus positive ones? There isn't; it's all just energy flowing regardless of outcome.

God wants us to be safe and happy—and gave us literally everything we need to create such an existence, including the intelligence to solve the inherent survival issues of this planet—but heaven will not live our lives for us. There would be no point to our existence in that case.

VISUALIZATION: ALIGNING YOUR THOUGHTS WITH LIMITLESSNESS

As discussed earlier, fear and intimidation about attracting certain things into your life are often the first and biggest blocks you face. When you look at something, and even give yourself permission to *visualize* it as a current reality, your mind starts to *accept* it as reality. Remember, while we as humans can be so focused on the physical aspects of our existence, everything is actually just energy. So, when we align the energy of our minds and souls with something, we become attuned to its vibration.

Arguably, science has theories that all energy is vibration. When I was young, a teacher told me, "If our thoughts are made of energy, and every molecule in everything around us is energy, why can't we attract whatever we want with our thoughts, when what we want is made of the same basic ingredients that we are?" I'll be honest—nothing was ever the same for me after hearing and pondering what he said. (Thanks, Chuck!)

In our minds, we tend to hold different manifestations on different pillars of varying height. Simple desires like finding a good seat at a restaurant, getting a parking spot, or not missing the bus are easy to process. It seems so straightforward for them to come true—the pillars are at our fingertips, so to speak—so why would we hesitate to wish for them?

Then the pillars get a little higher—maybe that car you want, perhaps the career you are dreaming of, or a love interest you have in mind. These things get a little trickier because you still have questions as to how you can achieve them. You ultimately have confidence that they will one day come true, but you fear they will be hard to accomplish.

Then we have even higher pillars, the ones that house the "holy grail" of dreams—often things like being wildly rich, being famous, or driving a Lamborghini. While you hold these dreams in your heart and mind, you also accept that they probably aren't realistic, for whatever logical or illogical reason, and for the most part won't actually happen. So now whatever is up on that pedestal is out of your reach, according to you.

What message do you think the universe and heaven hear when they see the way you've categorized your dreams? They see that you *really* want a good parking space, and you're pretty much detached from driving that sports car. So what comes true?

In order to manifest what makes you happy, you have to bring those pillars down; you have to level the playing field and let yourself believe that living the rest of your life on a yacht with your soul mate is exactly as achievable as finding a good seat on the bus. Energetically, those things don't differ at all to the universe. Energy will always take the path of least resistance, and everything you want is made of energy—so why would you resist your dreams?

Exercise: Leveling the Playing Field of Your Desires

Make a list of the things that you would want to have in life—everything from material objects to love to health to energy—and rank them in order from what you consider to be the easiest to the most difficult to achieve. What's interesting about that list is that if you showed it to anyone else, they would rank those same things, or any similar desires they might have, in a different order. We have a tendency to etherically pedestal our desires, based on our perception of them.

Everything is out there in the universal plane: that dream car, or that Miami apartment, or feeling a sense of belonging in life. What we are going to do is level the playing field with a visualization exercise. Because, according to heaven, there's no difference between manifesting one dollar . . . and being a published author of 100 books and changing the world. There is, energetically, no difference . . .

> *Visualize, in that universal plane, all the things you desire up on different pedestals, the heights dependent on how easy or difficult to achieve you might consider them to be in the moment. Take a breath and just feel the energy of everything that you're wanting in life in the now, or for the future, or for other people.*

> *Visualize all of the pedestals slowly sinking, as if losing hydraulic pressure, coming to*

your level . . . so that everything that you feel in your energy field as far as desires—soul, human, material, or spiritual—are concerned exist right here on this plane with you. The process of wrapping your mind around the fact that not one thing is more difficult to achieve than another can really help you energetically to start moving forward toward what it is you're supposed to do—not putting arbitrary limitations, or arbitrarily applying the brakes, on anything.

For every desire, you may have just assumed it takes "this much effort" and "this much time." It may, or it may not. It's not for you to determine now. Right now is for you to open your soul up to allow that energy, to allow these gifts, and to allow your birthright into your life.

God will always take care of the how. You have no idea whom you will meet, what doors will open, and what ideas or inspirations you'll have tomorrow. You have no idea what tomorrow will be like. Dream limitlessly, and know that the consistent dreams—the big dreams— are your soul calling.

There's no need to limit yourself because you think something is impossible. I love what Audrey Hepburn had to say about it: "Nothing is impossible; the word itself says 'I'm possible.'"

All quoting aside, with affirmative manifesting essentially what you're doing is taking the life of your dreams off the pedestal. By showing gratitude for it, you've brought the energy and the essence of what it is, what you're wanting to attract, to your level.

●————————————————————————————●

Vision Boards

Another great tool for bringing new things into your life is a vision board: a dedicated place, usually a wall or door, where you put images of what you want in life—houses, cars, stacks of money, couples in love, glorious destinations . . . you name it.

A vision board gets its power from psychological conditioning. The more time you spend in the energy of something, the more you condition yourself to its presence, and the less intimidated you are about it. I took *my* vision boards to the next level when I was manifesting a house back in 2004. I even let myself think about the day-to-day stuff like watering the lawn and repairing the garbage disposal. I *really* let myself live in that house before I even knew the address or how I could afford it. Then, a few months later, a Realtor literally knocked on the door of my apartment and said, "I will pay the fees to break your lease if you buy a house with me."

So I did, and after I moved in . . . the garbage disposal broke. Careful what you wish for.

My point is that far too many of us hold ourselves back from experiencing what we are meant to experience in life because we give up long before we start. Certain things in life seem so difficult to achieve that we often don't even try. They say that the best way to make God laugh is to plan; knowing the route isn't necessary, only the destination.

So please consider making a vision board—and when you're clipping out images or printing them from the Internet, do not limit yourself. If you feel hesitant to put something on your board, first have an honest discussion with yourself as to why. You'll often find that it is only the fear you can't achieve something that causes you to try to convince yourself you don't really want it.

I used to give a lot of angel readings about relationships, and a very common scenario I would hear about from people was that it's easier to attract a new partner once you already have a partner. For example, I was giving a reading to a man who said he was confused about why now that he had a girlfriend, suddenly girls seemed to find him more interesting or attractive. When he'd been single, he felt he couldn't get anyone to pay attention to him.

Not just in love but in many aspects of life, once you are familiar with something, it appears to be more achievable—it seems easier to improve upon what you have than it is to get it in the first place. A vision board allows you to experience the visual energy of your material dreams and desires so that they suddenly become within reach.

AFFIRMING WHAT YOU DESIRE

One of my earliest childhood memories is of walking past my mother's bedroom when she was getting ready for the day. I could hear her in her bathroom listening to and repeating words from an audio recording she had made of her own voice.

At this point my mother worked for an insurance company and had zero fame or public image—but the words on her recording said otherwise. I will never forget what I heard:

- "I am a published author."
- "I am abundant in all aspects of my life."
- "I help people, and people help me."
- "I travel and make a big, positive difference in this world."

At that age, I wasn't able to make a lot of sense of what I heard, but I was observant enough to know none of it was currently true. I used to hear my mother speak a lot about her plans in life and how she knew her life was going to be one of purpose.

I have clear memories of some of my mother's first classes, where she would have 5 or 10 people show up. Now it is normal for her classes to have over 500 attendees, sometimes close to 1,000. Why? Because people are waking up all over the world and want answers. While I believe angel classes can be an amazing experience, I am the first to say that no one needs them to connect with heaven and access divine guidance.

Looking back, it's very interesting to me to think about affirmations in general. In a way, an affirmation is a lie. It states something that is not yet true as if it were fact. Affirmations imply so much without taking the "how" or the "when" into consideration. In fact, according to the literal, mainstream way of thinking, affirmations are pure fantasy. Really, they are, if you think about it.

However, affirmations work. There is something about proclaiming an outcome—and repeating it until you believe it—that serves to somehow align you with that destiny.

How is that? How can our words be so powerful? How can a statement change our future?

It is because of exactly what I have said on many occasions: The universe brings us exactly what we want. The universe is very literal in its interpretations, so the more specific we can be with our affirmations, the better off we end up. Affirmations, and their clear and documented success rate, are proof of the malleability of our existence. They prove that we can live in whatever world we want.

Affirmations work in a two-step process:

1. The first and most essential step is to **believe in yourself**—and while this may not seem easy at first, I encourage you to create your own affirmation recording and don't hold back at all when you record it. Affirmations are your opportunity to play with what you may consider to be the limits of your dreams and hopes. Talk in present tense, as if everything you state is already here in your life. When you say out loud that you "will," it's powerful; when you say that you *are,* it's transformational. Please do not focus on how you sound. This is for you and you alone (unless you want to share it). Don't worry about the phrasing; the most essential guideline when creating your affirmation recording is to not hold back.

2. The second step is to **give yourself permission to believe the affirmations**. If you feel the energy of doubt, if you sense your mind wandering or becoming distracted (a very common tactic of the ego), or if you start thinking about the "how" or the "when," you need to actively push those sensations away. Stay focused and let your mind play with the energy of your affirmations and dreams. The more you do, the more natural it will feel.

Affirmations are not just a tool to help you achieve your dreams; I feel they are as essential as air and food if you feel that you have been holding yourself back in life. Affirmations teach us that the goal is far more important than the plan.

They also show us how, as powerful as we humans are, it can be harmful if we don't know how to properly deploy that power for our own good.

Nevertheless, we often feel so individually powerless to change the state of our world. One of the many common questions I get when I teach about manifesting with the angels is: "Is it wrong to use the power of affirmations or visualization to bring good things and/or material gain into our lives?" That's a very understandable question; I mean, is heaven here to help us, or are we here merely to serve, as stated in so many religious texts?

MANIFESTING FOR "PERSONAL GAIN" VS. "THE GREATER GOOD"

It has been thought for thousands of years, across many cultures, that wishing for more or achieving an abundant life was somehow wrong—or even a sin. For generations we humans have been taught either directly or indirectly to feel guilty whenever we find happiness or receive blessings, and as a result, far too many of us feel more comfortable if our lives match the status quo of those around us so we don't stick out or cause jealousy.

I will admit there is a certain comfort level in accepting your lot in life and not striving for higher than the norm. You know what to expect (for the most part), no one judges you, you don't have any heightened fears of "losing it all," and you don't risk alienating those around you and suffering the resulting loneliness.

Imagine . . .

Think about this in your own life: Take just a moment to sit back and allow yourself to imagine that literally everything you are currently seeking to manifest came true. You have the exact job you want, you live in the city you desire, you have the person in your life who meets your needs—everything is in complete and perfect alignment and all is how you would have it.

Now think about the people currently in your life: How are they affected by these changes? If you're thinking, *They are doing great, because in my dream I won the lotto and now I can buy them all houses and cars!* please move beyond that for a second. Think instead of you, as a being, living in complete fulfillment and happiness. Think about waking up in the morning and knowing exactly why you are alive. No longer do you question the purpose of your existence—instead you *live* it. Think about this honestly—how will this affect your relationships in life?

I can tell you from personal experience that although on the surface this sort of existence seems innocuous, it does, in fact, come with some interesting changes.

So when we call on angels to help us (remember, free will dictates that we must proactively ask for help) and when we open our hearts to the idea of living a purposeful life, changes begin. When our energy begins to rise as a result of this open relationship with the divine love of heaven, we start to become ultrasensitive to the energy we allow ourselves to be exposed to. We also start to become aware of our energetic effects on those around us.

The more time you spend in this higher vibration, the more acclimated you become to it, and, therefore, the easier it is for you to recognize situations, people, or places that do not resonate with you. This is part of how the changes keep coming, and when you find yourself in a situation where a long-standing relationship or friendship of any level of intimacy is at jeopardy, it's important to remember one thing— you're the one who has changed. And while it can be so easy to judge those around you who seemingly do not want to solve the issues they face by asking for help (which you know works), it's also important to consider that you may be in their lives for a reason, as a beacon lighting their path, modeling the power of possibility.

Since we can accept that heaven does want us all to be happy, it isn't a stretch to imagine that the messengers of heaven, the angels, have a very powerful role in helping us find happiness. Remember, our happiness is important: the more blessings we allow into our lives, the more we have to share with the world. When we hold ourselves back out of guilt (either because we were taught to feel guilty or we unfairly compare our blessings to other people's lives), we do the world a disservice, because we are perpetuating the same arbitrary lack mind-set that caused humanity to forget about our power and purpose in the first place. So, in the next chapter, we'll look more closely at the role of the angels in manifestation and the power of heaven to lift away our doubts and blocks.

Chapter 3

ASKING FOR
HELP FROM HEAVEN

I often think back to my own childhood—and although I was open to what my mother taught me about angels, I was also very skeptical that they were willing to help *me*. Why me?

For years and years, whenever I would complain to my mother about something in my life, she would always reply with the same words: "Ask the angels for help, and they will take care of everything."

There were times when I was so emotional about what I was complaining about that those words meant nothing to me. The idea of asking heaven for help seemed insufficient or ineffective. It seemed like the long and uncertain way of handling a problem—I wanted a solution now!

My mother never gave up, though. Even when I made it clear through my actions that she wasn't helping me when she told me to ask the angels, she never stopped saying those words.

And she easily could have. Think about it: Would you keep giving the same advice over and over to someone who openly and blatantly disregarded it? Probably not—so it goes without saying how immensely grateful I am for my mother's resolve and consistency.

You see, even though I didn't feel helped by her words or by the idea of asking the angels for assistance at the time, the truth is, I was still learning on a soul level from my exposure to her higher vibration. While my human mind insisted on maintaining control of my life—and my ego fears continued tricking me into believing that they had my best interests at heart—deep down I was running out of patience with this mind-set.

I watched my mother utterly transform her life. I remember when she was working as a psychotherapist, she was so stressed at times that she would pull the car over and just start crying. My brother, Grant, and I, being too small to get out of our car seats in the back, would just have to sit and watch and ask if she was okay. By listening to her angels and following her guidance, eventually she changed all of that. It was very obvious to us, even as children, that she was now truly happy, and although I didn't feel the calling at the time to talk to the angels, I could not deny the real and tangible improvements to my mother's life.

When I was around two years old, my mother and father were divorced. They are both very strong people, with no desire to give up on their children, so Grant and I spent almost our entire childhoods in a custody battle. We would spend one or two years with our father, then equal time with our mother.

What I personally found most impactful from the contrast of living with either parent was the spiritual aspect. My father and his entire side of the family are very Catholic. So I went to Catholic church and school and was even baptized. During my time in church, I was fascinated by stories about the angels. Every time I heard a Bible verse that spoke about heaven's direct interaction with humanity, I felt almost jealous. I would wonder, *Why not now? Why was all of this amazing, well-documented heavenly interaction limited to a time so long ago? Why is none of this happening today?*

Like most questions of this sort, I'm sure the Bible has an answer—but I was more interested in what people had to say about this. Most people in my church would reply, "Jesus will come back—be ready." I'm not here to bash traditional religion, but that never felt right to me. *"Be ready"? . . . I'm ready now!*

Since I felt unsatisfied with the answers I was receiving, I decided to just ask God. When I spoke directly to God, I could immediately feel this warm glow of loving energy wash over me. It felt so right and so divine that I knew I wasn't imagining it. I would ask God why angels don't talk to us anymore, and the answer I received blew me away: *The angels will spread My Word to anyone who asks for it.*

That changed everything for me—from that moment forward, I knew that what my mother kept telling me was right: heaven is love, and angels answer those who ask. So I began asking.

I asked God to help with the custody battle, as it was really hard on all of us—I instantly felt that same love and light wash over me, and I knew my prayers were heard. From that day on, I knew the truth: God wants us to be happy, God loves us unconditionally, and heaven is here to help us in life.

WHO ARE THE ANGELS?

Angels are all around us. Whether you know it or not, you are surrounded by etheric beings who want to help you. In fact, their very purpose for being around you is to help.

Angels are the embodiment of God's energy sent from heaven to be with us our entire lives. Before we are born, we set out a life plan for ourselves pertaining to the lessons we are meant to learn on a soul level. This life plan contains exactly what, where, and with whom we are meant to be. Nothing is more fulfilling than being on course with your life purpose, or plan. It does not matter if you set out to be a millionaire yacht owner, a small-business owner, or a parent of beautiful children. Living according to how you planned this lifetime before you were born is the greatest accomplishment you can achieve. Just know that there definitely is a plan for you, and the angels are present to remind you of this fact because your soul is yearning for its true purpose.

There are two types of angels: *guardian angels* and *archangels*.

- **Guardian angels** are around each of us. When we are born, we are given

no fewer than two guardian angels.
These angels serving in this way are
assigned to be with us our entire lives
and offer their loving and divine help,
plus guidance and support according
to what we have set out to do. The
guidance you receive from your
guardian angels has a lot to do with the
lessons you have set up for yourself. As
you live and grow, you take on more
and more guardian angels, especially in
times when you need, want, or ask for
help in your life. Most guardian angels
stay with us for the duration of our lives
once they come to be with us.

- **Archangels** also surround us.
  Archangels are larger and more
  powerful than our guardian angels,
  and while each archangel is capable
  of anything, certain archangels have
  chosen to specialize. What this means
  to you is that according to what issue,
  question, concern, triumph, or decision
  you face, there is an archangel that
  loves to help in that exact situation.

Each archangel also has an aura color representing the frequency at which the angel vibrates. Every frequency of energy—spiritual, angelic, earthly, and human—has a unique color combination. Archangels serve as a direct connection to our higher power and as the voice of the Creator.

The reason we have angels is to help us find and maintain the course of our life path. Angels help to take care of the details, timing, and the "dirty work" of the decisions and problems we face in life.

By opening yourself up to the power and love of the angels around you, you not only make your life easier, as it was meant to be, but you also make the angels very happy that your soul is once again in touch with their presence and guidance.

You see, communicating with angels is completely natural, and built into every human who ever was, or ever will be. It is how we were designed; there is a constant energetic connection between humanity, heaven, and the angels that can never be severed. The angels are here to help us in any aspect of our lives, limited only by our own imaginations. So when you ask, *How can I open up the channel between my angels and me?* it is important to know that this is less about learning than it is about remembering.

Whether you know it or not, the angels are communicating with you every day of your life. They're showing you signs, working with your intuition, offering you guidance, and giving you information in the form of gut feelings. Anytime in your life that you have been in a predicament where you found a resolution, or the situation magically fixed itself, the angels were hard at work. The angels will always help us cope with, navigate through, and ultimately learn from any given situation, good or bad.

Think of signs as bread crumbs down the path of our lives. Signs are not only designed to guide us through the twists and turns of our lives, but also to confirm that we are still on that life path. At the very least, a sign will always serve as a confirmation that you are on the right path, even if that's not currently apparent.

Every call, aspiration, manifestation, or wish that we have, especially the consistent ones, are divinely sent to us. The feelings of yearning we get are reminders sent from our angels that we are meant to do so much more in this lifetime. What this means to you is that dreams and wishes about bettering your life are real, sanctioned by God, and very much possible to achieve as you learn to let go of fear.

What we can do to begin feeling, hearing, and seeing the angels is to first affirm our openness to it. There are no magic potions or sacred rituals necessary to ask the angels into our lives. If we are in a blocked state right now, it's because for one reason or another, we chose to ignore or shut out guidance.

To affirm your openness to having the angels once again participate in your life in an interactive way, please consider saying so aloud or in your mind:

"Angels, I allow myself to once again be open to your presence. I allow myself to be open to the gifts of heaven in the form of your divine and loving guidance. I understand that you are here to help me in every aspect of my life, no matter how big or small. I hereby undo and release any and all actions or decisions that may have blocked my openness and sensitivity to your messages. I ask you to please come back into my life, and I have openness to the guidance of heaven."

Really allow yourself to feel the energy of these words, or your own version of them. The angels want to interact with you, and often just ask that you take the first step. Open your heart and mind to the idea that there's a force in this universe that wants you to be happy.

Now that we have resolved to reawaken our connection with the angels—yes, it really is that easy—it's just a matter of waiting for the undeniable messages and signs to pour into our lives. If you're wondering if there's anything else you could do to increase the speed and clarity of the angels' messages, you're in luck. Like with most of our natural abilities, practice makes perfect, and the more we know about ourselves, the more refined, clear, and connected we can feel.

We deserve happiness, purpose, and fulfillment in our lives, so let's stop delaying our purpose and ask the angels to guide us to our next step in life!

DISPELLING DOUBT

In my line of work, I talk with people of all walks of life. I obviously meet spiritual people—but I also meet a lot who would not consider themselves to be open to talking to angels. The most common reason I hear is that they feel that it won't work . . . that it won't help them, because this is all make-believe. I can relate. I spent a portion of my childhood also questioning. The funny thing about it, though, is that heaven and the angels do not ask us to either be 100 percent spiritual or 100 percent nonspiritual—we aren't binary creatures. Unfortunately, some traditional religions have perpetuated this misconception that we can be either completely on board or not at all—and the truth lies somewhere in between.

Whenever anyone asks me for advice on opening up to the angels, I always tell them the same thing: "No one can ever convince you of the authenticity of heaven and God's love for us—nor would any human ever be saddled by heaven with such a task." Instead, all heaven and the angels ask from us is for an opportunity to prove their authenticity to us. It really is heaven's job to prove this, and heaven will do exactly that, quite enthusiastically and beyond a measure of doubt, for anyone who asks.

PROOF POSITIVE

When we open our hearts and minds to great, positive change, the first step is asking heaven to come into our lives and guide us to happiness and purpose. The only difference between your current life and the one you desire is the incremental changes that must occur—that's it!

When we ask heaven for help, the angels immediately get to work by guiding us to become aware of what is not currently serving our purpose and by giving us an opportunity to change or heal these aspects. Heaven will always send us signs and reminders that we are on the right path and that our efforts are justified.

Heaven is the best cheerleader and mascot you could hope for. If you ever doubt that, ask for a sign, proof that angels are with you and that positive change is coming. Be clear and confident with your prayers, never feel guilty asking for exactly what you need, and certainly don't ever allow yourself to believe the myth that there is such a thing as asking for too much.

It's very important that we not humanize the angels and assume the same limitations we have pertain to them. God and the angels never get tired of our prayers and requests. They do not get frustrated if we aren't following their guidance, and, most important, heaven never gives up on us.

Asking is often the easiest and simultaneously the hardest step to take. Many people refuse to ask heaven for help because they are afraid that doing so would prove that it doesn't work—and they aren't yet prepared to live with the magnitude of a reality like that. But it does work—and requires no penance or adherence to a different set of beliefs.

God does not want to challenge or change us beyond that which must change in order for us to align ourselves with the purpose we came here to live. There is no risk or obligation in asking heaven to prove itself to you—there is nothing to fear about asking the angels to help you in life.

So please live your spiritual life without guilt, free of fear of judgment or persecution, because heaven is on your side. Be open to the voice and guidance of heaven and never allow a problem to dwell in your heart or mind without sharing it with the loving and helpful angels by your side. The question should no longer be whether it's too much to ask angels to bring happiness into your life—instead, it is, are you asking *enough*?

TALKING TO ANGELS

As I've said, there is no ritual involved in talking to the angels. I like to think of the angels as the voice of—or an extension of—God's energy. While many of us have been taught that we must be humble in the presence of the Lord, if you actually talked to God about this instead of listening to other humans, you might discover an interesting truth, as I have.

God is the source of everything and, of course, should be treated with the same respect we would want to be shown—but our Creator does not require worship or servitude. Nor does God expect us to proclaim that we are not worthy of heaven's love, guidance, and blessings. For a long time, traditional religion extolled the virtues of fearing God, but we now live in the age of awakening where we can allow ourselves to feel the limitless and condition-free love of God, instead. Living in fear of God makes no sense.

Traditional, fear-based religion served a very important role in the evolution of our planet. Society as we know it is based on the same, "fear the consequences but strive for the promises" mantra that once offered very clear parameters to live within. The fear of hell and the promise of heaven lent a sense of accountability to societies that otherwise would have lived lawlessly.

I thank traditional religion for keeping the awareness of God and the angels (and other masters and guides) in front of us. However, the age of fearing

God is coming to an end. It no longer serves our planet to limit each other and ourselves because we are afraid of heaven's wrath.

Who suffers when everyone is happy? No one. When each of us wakes up to this fact, there will be no more questions about the love of God and heaven. When we actually talk to God and find out for ourselves that the divine does not care about our sexual orientation, how often we attend church, or our spiritual trappings, it is then that we can form a personal and loving relationship with our Creator. I encourage you to find all of this out for yourself.

WHY DO ANGELS EXIST?

When I asked God why the angels exist, I really loved the answer I received. God explained to me that His energy is so high and pure that it is often difficult to feel confident we can hear His answer when we ask from a place of strong emotions. The angels basically exist here on this planet with us to translate the Word of God into a language that we can understand, regardless of what energetic state we are in. The angels are the part of God that can match our human vibration such that the messages heaven has for us can be easily understood in most situations. It doesn't matter if you're an angry person or a happy person—you have complete clarity when talking to angels. Angels make the guidance of heaven more easily accessible—and if you really think about it, the angels are like our etheric teammates on this planet.

When I ask the angels if they ever get tired of hearing our complaints and prayers, I get a resounding *No!* They will never get tired of hearing what we need, because they share the same goals we humans do: furthering our purpose and happiness. I truly believe that the purpose of life, in this current state of evolution, is to reconnect with our hearts, learn to live without fear, and accept that we are meant to be happy.

I don't expect you to believe any of this just because you're reading it here. Instead, I again strongly encourage you to test it by forming your own relationship with God and the angels. The age of fear and control are over, the age of purpose and happiness is upon us, and if you ask for help finding this out for yourself, I know that you will be as enthusiastic about it as I am.

Chapter 4

ANSWERED PRAYERS

Let me explain a bit more about angelic guidance and exactly the way it is designed. The angels want us to feel good and confident about following our guidance. Sure, at times the guidance the angels give us will confront our inward fears—but outwardly when angels guide us, we can be sure that is a safe path to follow.

Fear is so harmful because, as I've said many times, all energy we allow to resonate within ourselves is part of what we manifest. We have a divine responsibility to match our inner energy with our outward desires. I have found that one of the best ways to get past fear and ego is through trust and prayer. Those may sound ineffective or insufficient, but please allow me to explain.

First of all, as long as you know that fear is 100 percent normal and that heaven will never judge you for experiencing it, you're off to a good start. No need to add guilt to an already low energy.

The second thing you should know about angelic guidance is that it's literally impossible to miss a message. No matter how casual or critical the guidance, the angels will always find a way to get you the message—even if they recruit another human to give it to you. So, as long as you know that you can't miss a message, you can be sure that the ones you have received up to this moment are all you need for now.

If you are praying for further guidance or clarity and have not yet received it, just trust—because it will come. It actually takes a lot more effort to ignore the angels than to hear their messages. This is because when the angels want you to know something or take action, they will never stop telling you. So if you're getting guidance to, for example, move to a new city and start a new job (as we talked about before) and you have natural, logical, and normal fears about making a move like this—what should you do? Yes, *pray.*

THE POWER OF PRAYER

Praying is essential at this step in manifestation, because you already know what you want to do or are guided to do—now it's a matter of the all-important "how" and "when." When you spend time worrying about all that can go wrong, you're inviting those things to happen.

That's why I always say that God-given free will is such a big responsibility. God basically says, *You can do whatever you want—but if you* want *to be happy, only* do *what you want.* This "doing" also includes what you think about and the energy you allow yourself to dwell in.

When you keep praying for the same thing, you accomplish several feats:

- You spend less time worrying about it.

- You keep your energy aligned with it.

- You affirm to heaven that you are ready for it.

- You invoke messages to help you with the "how" and "when."

When we pray for something, it is basically reinforcing that we really want it—and since heaven is by our side and also wants us to be happy, the angels get to work on our behalf.

What the angels showed me to help explain the way guidance works is this: Our "being" (mind, body, and soul) is like a car, with one driver's seat. *We* get to decide who occupies that seat. When we pray to God and ask for help with our purpose, we are essentially offering up that seat to heaven. We allow God and the angels to then guide us by giving us signs, intuitive "hits," heavenly messages, and sometimes fortuitous "chance" encounters.

As long as we keep an open heart and mind and follow our guidance, we keep that seat open to heaven. However, the second we decide to take over the navigation of our path by overthinking, going into fear or doubt, and dwelling in that mentality, heaven will take a back seat.

Prayer for Guidance

If you feel comfortable piloting your own vessel, there is nothing wrong with that. But if you feel you could use some help, clarity, and guidance in life, you have instant access to that by just asking.

Try it now; please relax and say something like the following silently in your mind:

"Heaven, in this moment I ask you to please come into my life and help me to find my divine purpose. Angels, I ask you to work with me in every aspect of my life to give me the messages, guidance, and signs that will lead me to my reason for being on this planet. I affirm definitively that from this moment forward, I choose a happy life full of fulfillment. I choose to know why I am here and live my life accordingly. Angels, I ask you to please work with me through my daily life and to walk with me every step I take."

Once you say a prayer like this, the next magic step isn't learning to hear the angels—they will always find a way to communicate with you through signs, via your intuition, and by presenting new opportunities. The magic lies, rather, in learning to stay loyal to your new commitment by refusing to allow fear or doubt to take over your thoughts. When you feel afraid, impatient, or uncertain, instead of racking your brain to try to find answers, just pray.

"Let go and let God" is such a popular phrase for good reason. The more we let go—the more we make efforts to distract ourselves from thinking about the "how"—the more our minds remain open to the "what" that heaven will show us with very persistent and unmistakable signs.

SIGNS FROM ABOVE

A sign is anything that distracts your attention away from whatever you were doing or focusing on in a given moment. Signs can take any form, ranging from hearing song lyrics that coincide with what you're praying about, to seeing a feather in an unlikely place. There is no set formula of "If you see this, it means that" with signs. Rather, I like to say, "If you have to ask whether it's a sign, it probably is."

The angels answer most prayers by giving you signs and other forms of divine guidance (such as intuitive feelings or repetitive ideas) if you take the following steps:

1. **Ask.** Remember that the angels can only give you signs if you request them.

2. **Notice the signs when they occur.** Related to this is trusting the signs aren't coincidental. If you doubt the validity of the ones you come across, repeat #1 above and ask for a sign that what you're receiving is real.

3. **Follow through on the guidance imparted by the signs.** If your angels' sign asks you to take action, then you

must do so before your prayer can be
fulfilled. When you notice and follow
the sign, all the doors of opportunity
and peacefulness subsequently open.

All signs have meaning. Sometimes the meaning
is obvious and literal; other times the meaning may
not seem clear—but at the bare minimum, a sign will
always mean you're on the right path and the angels
are with you. If a sign doesn't seem to have any other
meaning, its message is just that simple. Just adopt a
"steady as she goes" approach and stay the course.

When you learn about divine timing in the next
chapter, hopefully you'll come to agree with me that
getting a sign that you're on the right path—even if
your life is not how you would like it to be—is amazing, because you know that great, positive change
is coming, and will happen exactly when the time is
right, when you are energetically ready.

When you receive these signs, take a minute to
allow yourself to feel grateful, to feel fulfilled by the
fact that no matter what it is that you envision for
your future, right now could not and should not be
any different. You're exactly where you're supposed
to be, which is a divine confirmation that, whatever

it is that you're working for, whatever it is that you're manifesting in your life, is on its way.

GUIDANCE FROM ABOVE

Obviously, if we could all completely trust that the changes we are called to make are divinely guided and following through could never sabotage our lives, it would be great. But heaven does not expect us to be ready for wholesale change all at once.

In fact, you may be surprised to hear that although heaven is immensely eager for us to wake up to our purpose, we will never be expected to rush. There is no ticking timer, no race—no reason to push yourself beyond what you can handle in any given moment. That's part of the beauty of working with heaven.

Angels don't get paid by the hour, so there is no need to overcomplicate our relationship with them by feeling the obligation to follow all of our guidance right away when we receive it. Much of the time when we get a message that we are meant to make a big change, nothing at all is immediately expected of us except an awareness that the message is present and valid.

A lot of heavenly messages are ignored because when we receive the guidance that we are supposed to be doing something different in life, we become frightened, confused, or overwhelmed, and have no idea how to follow it. We disregard it or perhaps pay an angel reader to help us make more sense of it.

Let me save you a lot of time and money right now—heaven knows us very, very well. God and the angels know exactly what state of mind we are in at any given moment, and they know exactly how we will respond to the guidance they give us.

Preparatory vs. Divine Guidance

Oftentimes, we are meant to receive messages calling for change merely as preparation for that upcoming change. Too many of us are afraid that if we don't act at once, we may miss out on a great opportunity—but this simply is not what is going on.

So there are two very different kinds of guidance: (1) *preparatory guidance*, which we just discussed; and (2) *divine guidance*. Both are divine in their own way, but true divine-guidance messages are the ones where you just *know* now is the time to act—and you usually will do exactly that.

Heaven knows when you will take action and when you aren't yet ready for it; please trust that. If you receive intuitive guidance, repetitive signs, or a direct message to make a big change that you feel you can't do, then *don't*. Just acknowledge that you received the message (it never hurts to thank heaven for it) and ask for further signs and guidance to help you follow this guidance.

Heaven will never ask you to do something before you are completely ready—and while you may never feel completely ready to make certain changes, when it is the divine time to do so, you will know beyond a doubt. This should clear up a lot of confusion—if you receive a message that you have no idea how to act on, don't.

I meet too many people who immediately quit their jobs, move to a new city, and find themselves overwhelmed and lost. Heaven would never put us in that situation, and while it can pose a challenge to tell the difference between preparatory and divine guidance, asking heaven to clarify beyond a doubt will always work.

Remember, there is literally no limit to how much you can ask for and how often you can ask for it. If any aspect of working with heaven brings confusion . . .

- . . . first, know that is very normal; and

- . . . second, simply ask heaven to help you to gain clarity.

When the time is right to move forward and make changes in your life, you will know it.

BEING OPEN TO THE UNEXPECTED

When we can fully accept that heaven will always guide us to *where* we are meant to be, *when* it is meant to be, and that we *will* find our purpose there, it is then that we are completely ready to awaken to the divine reason we chose to come into this life.

There will always be an answer to our prayers, but it may not always come wrapped in the packaging we were expecting, or follow the timelines we demand. The answer may take the form of a more fitting option, but oftentimes it is one we weren't thinking of. So if we don't realize that this was, in fact, an answer, we may feel as if the angels are not hearing us. However, I can assure you that it will bring you exactly the lasting happiness you desire.

As I said before, we can sometimes become too focused on a specific thing or situation, convinced that it is the only answer to our prayers and our sole mode of happiness. Remembering that the ultimate experience is what is important—never limit your dreams because they seem impossible or improbable. Maybe you are convinced that Brad Pitt is your soul mate; who is to tell you otherwise? Pray for that! But please keep an open mind, because while you have used Brad Pitt as the embodiment of what you desire, heaven sees what really matters to your heart.

So even if you instead meet someone else, that does not mean that the relationship you create with that person will not *feel* exactly like what you were praying for. If you're manifesting a new job, keep focused on what you want, but trust that heaven may just know you a bit better than you know yourself, and stay open to what might appear to be a different opportunity than what you were first expecting.

Heaven, of course, delivers on our specific prayers as well. Don't ever allow yourself to believe that unanswered prayers exist. Prayers are *always* answered, and the more we take divine timing into consideration, the more we will come to believe this.

UNBURDENING YOURSELF TO HEAVEN

As you've read repeatedly in this book, prayer is the key to opening your heart and mind to happiness. It is the key to allowing heaven into your life to help guide you along your path to purpose. Prayer also allows you the opportunity to unload the weight of your pain, fears, and excuses.

When we pray, we fine-tune our energy to be focused specifically on the topic at hand. Our minds then release the clutter of worry, obligations, and general life distractions so that our hearts and souls can align to focus on what is most important to us.

Prayer does not have to be ritualistic; you can pray from literally any position. You can pray with your eyes open or closed. You can pray while you're eating, working, jogging, or getting ready in the morning. There is no wrong way to pray.

However you prefer to pray, though, please ensure you do not add limitations when you speak to God. Pray limitlessly, pray from a completely open heart—pray knowing that you deserve to be happy. Most important, pray because our world can use as much happiness as it can get. Let your life be one of the conduits heaven uses to bring joy to our planet.

Should you ask heaven and the angels to help you in your life? Yes. Should you ever limit or use moderation in your prayers? No. Why would you?

There is every advantage to waking up to the magnificence of heavenly guidance; when you find happiness, the world becomes a happier place. The angels love us so much and want to see us smile, so please let them into your life and stay faithful that the guidance you receive is meant to direct you toward, and help you stay on, your path of purpose.

As we will explore in the next chapter, a lot of times when we feel that our prayers are unanswered, it really comes down to timing. It's normal and natural to want what we want, when we want it (or feel we need it), but often lessons and growth are necessary for us to be able to awaken to our next step in life.

Divine timing, as it's called, is proof that there is an inherent order underlying the chaos in the world and that there are angels guiding us each small step of the way, without overwhelming us with the magnitude of the big-picture trajectory all at once.

Chapter 5

DIVINE TIMING

Manifesting is about accepting what is while staying open to what can be. While the laws of the universe dictate that our thoughts will control our future, there is more than one force at play, which can make things appear confusing to people just starting out on their spiritual paths. This chapter outlines the importance of divine timing, helping you to understand that there will always be an answer to your prayers, but it may not always come in the sequence you were expecting.

DIVINE TIMING, DEFINED

Probably one of the most important, but sometimes frustrating and misunderstood, aspects of manifestation, *divine timing* states that everything that is meant to happen will happen when the time is right. It does not imply that fate and destiny rule our lives—divine timing works alongside our free will. Rather, divine timing tells us that there are certain points in our lives where we are more or less ready for change or finding our next step. There is a lot divine timing can teach us about life, and even about ourselves—and the more we understand the rules and dynamics behind this proverbial "universal queuing system," the easier it is for us to understand the spiritual evolution of humanity.

Depending on the situation—and your interpretation of the urgency of said situation—divine timing can feel like a roadblock. Knowing that certain aspects of life will not come to fruition until it is exactly the right time can sometimes be a tad demoralizing (to put it lightly).

No matter how patient we consider ourselves to be, I can guarantee you that every human on earth is impatiently waiting for at least one aspect of life to change in a positive way—it is the nature of our being. We as humans constantly strive to better our lives and surroundings, and from time to time we encounter a life aspect that needs to be changed *now*, if not yesterday.

For a long time I considered the whole dynamic of divine timing to be frustrating and pointless—I mean, why can't the good changes just happen *now*? Why do we have to wait to experience what we are praying for? God wants me to be happy, right?

Let's explore divine timing a bit and see what it has to teach us . . .

LESSONS IN DIVINE TIMING

It is pretty well understood and agreed upon by those who work with God and the angels that heaven does want us to be happy. Heaven wants us to not only live happy, purposeful lives but also to be able to *sustain* this happiness.

In order to make purpose, fulfillment, and happiness permanent fixtures in our lives, we must get to the point where we have learned the appropriate lessons, where we have experienced the necessary growth, so that the positive changes stick.

I like to think of it sort of like a rehearsal for the next step in your life. If you think about it, do you want positive change to debut now . . . or when the time is right, knowing beyond a doubt that it will be rave-reviews successful?

What divine timing tells us is that when we are ready, positive change will come. This does not mean happiness in general will be delayed; heaven will always provide for us while we prepare for our next step. I have learned over the years to embrace and appreciate divine timing, as it protects us from manifesting certain things too quickly, before we are truly ready for them.

As long as you maintain the faith that heaven is on your side and the answers to your prayers are coming, you will see exactly what I mean. When positive steps forward do occur in your life, you will see that they simply could not have happened any earlier or later.

DIVINE TIMING AND FREE WILL

Now, while all of that is easy to understand on paper, how is divine timing going to bring you comfort when you need a job right away? How is divine timing going to bring you companionship when you're lonely and ready to allow love into your life?

Well, just because we may not feel the ultimate answer to our prayers is present in our lives does not mean heaven does not hear us—and it certainly does not mean heaven is ignoring us. God-given free will dictates that we will attract what we think about—we have the freedom to create our own reality. When we assume that our prayers aren't being answered, it's very easy to miss the answers that *are* coming. We may not have any idea of what opportunities heaven is guiding us toward, but just because we can't see the big picture does not mean we aren't being heard.

When you work with heaven on a daily basis—asking for help, signs, and guidance—you'll never be left without what you need to survive and find happiness along the way. This may not be the most exciting news if you are waiting, but please trust heaven. Even if the time is not right for you to graduate to a new aspect of life, it does not mean you're meant to live an uninspired life in the meantime.

Heaven always has gifts in store for us, if we ask. The problem is that too many of us assume that if we can't get exactly what we are praying for, then something went wrong, somehow heaven doesn't hear us, or maybe we aren't meant to have whatever it is we are manifesting. This couldn't be further from the truth.

This is where the whole aspect of heavenly guidance gets really fun. We humans (whether we want to admit it or not) often maintain an all-or-nothing mentality when dealing with our manifestations. We often assume that we will not be satisfied with any alternative outcome. We do this because our human brains have a very convincing way of tricking us into believing we always know what is best for us in any given moment. Generally this isn't a bad thing—but there are times when heaven wants us to keep a more open mind about what tomorrow should contain.

Your job, soul mate, house, purpose—whatever you seek—*is* coming, but the path you're on may not have caught up to the actual experience yet.

What heaven asks of us during these transitional periods is to:

- first, maintain our faith (not only in heaven, but in ourselves); and

- second, keep praying and visualizing.

The more we ask, the more we are guided to move forward on our path (even if we don't realize progress is taking place) and the closer we get to our answered prayers. When we take guided actions to stay on our path, we can always find happiness and peace in knowing beyond a doubt that the answer to our prayers is coming—our path, by definition, is the road to our purpose.

So if you know you're on that path, how can you want anything else other than what you're currently experiencing?

TRUSTING DIVINE TIMING

I always find it so ironic when I look back on my life, especially at the uncertain times when I wasn't sure if what I wanted would ever become my reality. I now realize that what I went through to eventually *get* to where I wanted to be had everything to do with what I needed in order to *stay* there.

Even while our dreams appear to be pending, what we need in order to stay on our path will always be provided. Whether it's money, food, shelter, or companionship—if we refuse to give up just because the big answer hasn't arrived, we stay open to receiving these things, and as a result, we *will*. The second we throw up our hands and say, "This isn't working!" what do you think heaven hears? When we stop wishing and praying for something, we are telling heaven and the universe we no longer want it.

This is the point when so many of us get into trouble. We lose patience and faith because the path forward seems unclear or outright blocked—and we decide it's easier to pay attention to what we feel we *can* control. This is always a pivotal moment in our manifestations, and I encourage you not to give up like this.

Whenever you feel panicked that your prayers won't be answered in time, whenever you feel tired of waiting, or whenever you feel like giving up on your dreams—instead of stewing on all of this internally, hand these fears and concerns over to heaven. Ask the angels to show you a clear sign that what you're manifesting is, in fact, part of your divine purpose, and ask for proof it is coming. You'll be blown away by how clear and immediate these signs will come if you stay faithful.

MEANT TO BE

I couldn't have started teaching any sooner than I did; it was perfectly divinely timed. The angels wanted me to exhaust all possible alternatives so I could focus exclusively on my purpose without wondering what else I could be—especially when I was feeling too terrified to teach. They did that job so well that it's undeniable to me how trustworthy divine timing is.

It's normal to become impatient, especially when we think about the way heaven works in the context of the experiences we have with humans. Heaven has a plan—most of us can accept that—but what we often have trouble understanding is just how ingenious that plan is. Heaven knows us better than we know ourselves, and while we sometimes sit around nursing disappointment, wondering why our prayers aren't being answered, heaven is trying to remind us that they *are* being answered—but not always according to the timelines we assume they should follow. Nor do the answers always follow the "logical" path we assume they should.

The second you open your heart and mind to live a life of purpose, heaven gets to work. You might ask for a soul mate and suddenly be guided to do something that your logical mind assumes has absolutely nothing to do with love—but can you really be so sure?

While divine timing does play an essential role in the rapidity of the outcome to our prayers, this does not mean the angels expect us to live our lives mustering blind faith day after day—in fact, the opposite is true. The angels are always around us and will at any moment offer us confirmation that we are headed in the right direction, emotional comfort, and clear messages to help us down our path—all we need to do is ask.

LET "IT" COME TO YOU

And so in determining if something is right for you, you have to allow, accept, and appreciate that exploration is part of the process. The exploration is just as important as the destination.

As my mother and I have said so many times, prayer will always bring answers. Sometimes they'll come right away. And a lot of times they'll come progressively through life. Through signs. Through gut feelings. Through the consistency of what it is you're getting as guidance.

Sometimes you might realize that what you considered your purpose was actually you running away from something that you didn't like—*My purpose is to be powerful because I'm tired of not feeling powerful*—when in actuality that wouldn't satisfy your soul. In actuality, that would only satisfy your ego. So be careful.

To make sure that you are following what it is that your soul is here to do, you've got to allow yourself to take things step-by-step. Every time I get a new idea, a new inspiration, what I start off by doing is to ask the angels, *If this is divine, if this is what I'm meant to do, then please show me a clear and recognizable, undeniable sign.* And then I just let it go.

Human timing and the human sense of urgency doesn't always mesh with heaven's clock. And so that doesn't mean that you won't get an answer right away. But it does mean that the more you push for an answer, the more probable it is that you'll push it away. Or you might end up answering yourself with your ego.

So let that undeniable sign come. You get these divine messages when you least expect them because when you least expect something, that's when you're the least in control. Sometimes you have to step aside and allow a higher power than you, all-seeing both in the world and in time and the future, to take control. Sometimes relaxing can be the hardest thing to do. When you say, *Here, you take the wheel. I'm going to follow signs as they come, but until then I'm just going to live my life and go through my routine*, you will be absolutely amazed by how quickly the angels will start to make a difference.

The best, most honest way forward is to allow yourself to be guided. And this could take 24 hours; it could take 24 months—it all depends on that gestation period of whatever it is meant to be. And you wouldn't *want* to act before it's time to do so because it wouldn't be as meaningful. It wouldn't have the same impact on you, whomever it is you're trying to help, or whatever it is you're trying to bring into the world.

Meditation: Let Go and Let God

I love to use a meditation that I actually guide myself through to help organize my thoughts, separate my higher self from my lower self, and make sure that what it is I'm pursuing, what I *want* to do, is actually what I'm *guided* to do and not some sort of escape, not running away from something in my life that I don't currently like. As I've explained before, there's a difference between going to where you're divinely led and escaping from something that doesn't work for you.

The following is a very simple exercise, and I'd love for you to try it:

Please close your eyes, and I'm going to ask you to take a deep breath in. And just let yourself feel that breath. Sometimes when I inhale, I say "breath in, stress out." I breathe in so much that there's no more room for stress in my body. And I feel any sense of anticipation fall away from me . . .

If your palms are sweating and you're thinking, I really want to figure this out, *you've got to let that go. Even for a moment. Energy will always follow the path of least resistance, and that's not only a fact in physics, it's a fact in spirituality. And so the more relaxed we can allow our bodies to be and the more relaxed we can let our spirit be, the more energy will go through us.*

And so let the power of breath release from you any sense of anticipation, any fear, any so-called logical questions, any doubts. Let your breath completely relax your body. And just let that energy of the universe and of the angels and of pure divine guidance begin to flow through you.

And as you connect with this higher vibration, begin to allow yourself to experience the freedom of just being in the moment. As you allow yourself to just let go of the weight of all of your expectations—and the world's expectations—we're going to call in heaven. And what I mean is that we're going to call in anyone we feel guided to work with, be it your spirit guide, an ascended master, an archangel, or any other being that you feel comfortable working with. They are all connected to the same source.

And just allow yourself to feel your own energy around you. This is all a process of letting go. This is a process of letting your energy begin to rise as you surround yourself with this heavenly vibration and invite it into your being. And as you feel yourself fill with that light, allowing your body to remain completely relaxed, say: "Today I choose purpose. Today I affirm that my life will contain purpose. Fulfillment, peace, and happiness. Heaven, I accept this energy. I accept that I have guidance. Heaven, I ask you to please help me in this moment to discern: Is this guidance divine? Please use my body as an instrument of communication, heaven, and allow me to feel, to know, to see, and to hear clearly if this is the direction that I am meant to go in."

And just take a moment now and think about this possibility. Think about this idea. Don't think about how. Just think about "it." And just let yourself be there. Let yourself step inside and feel that energy: If I go in this direction, this is what my life will feel like. How does this feel?

Again, let's pray: "Heaven, I ask that you continue to work with me. In my everyday life, please show me consistent and clear messages as to whether this is the path I'm meant to follow or if there is a path that is more in line with my soul's purpose."

And then you just let go. We start with letting go. We set our intention. We ask for help, and we end with letting go.

While all angels, operating with divine timing, are able to help with manifestation and life purpose, there are certain angels with specialties and unique vibrations that can help us clear the road to happiness with ease.

In the next chapter, we are going to learn about Archangel Nathaniel, who is one of the most incredible energies I have worked with to help me know which changes I need to make in my life in order to move forward positively. Nathaniel has such an easy and automatic quality about his energy that I believe you'll come to know him and be as excited about his "block-clearing" ways as I am.

PART II

CLEARING BLOCKS AND ATTRACTING HAPPINESS, PURPOSE, AND FULFILLMENT WITH THE ANGELS

Chapter 6

HARNESSING THE POWER OF YOUR INNER PASSION WITH ARCHANGEL NATHANIEL

Nathaniel is a relatively unknown archangel. A student in Lucerne, Switzerland, first introduced me to Nathaniel in 2008. During one of the breaks in class, she asked me why I didn't talk more about this powerful angel. Truth be told, I had never heard of Archangel Nathaniel and informed her as much.

However, in the days and weeks following class, I couldn't seem to get Nathaniel out of my mind. I had a deep curiosity about him. Who was he? How could he help humankind? What messages did he have for *me*? I scoured the Internet but came up empty-handed. There was little to no information about Archangel Nathaniel available online at that time.

So I did what I always advise people to do when they have questions about an angel—go to the source. Ask the angel or being who they are, what messages they have, and what purpose they serve on this planet. I called upon Nathaniel and got to know him personally. And what I discovered forever changed my views on manifesting and angelic interaction.

THE ENERGY OF NATHANIEL

Nathaniel is an angel like no other. He has a vibrant, youthful energy that sets him apart from other angels of my experience. I like to think of Nathaniel as a remover of obstacles. When we manifest, a big part of the challenge we encounter comes from our doubts. These doubts act as obstacles on our path; they prevent us from reaching our goals and cause many of us to simply give up. Our doubts can be deeply hidden in our subconscious or known to us. When our doubts are hidden, they are especially challenging.

For example, let's say that you're trying to manifest a wonderful new career. You know that you want to be self-employed and feel in your heart that you're on the right track. All of your guidance confirms it. However, you continually run into problems, like missed opportunities and blocks, preventing you from realizing your desires. Because, unbeknownst to you, your doubts and fears are so deeply hidden that you are faced with the obstacles they place in your path with no clear way to overcome them.

Archangel Nathaniel has a way of helping you get to the root of your blocks. He helps you identify precisely what's holding you back and gives you clear guidance on how to remove it from your life.

Knowing how to overcome obstacles when we manifest is crucial to our success. It would be wonderful if our paths were always clear and it were only a matter of focusing our energy on our dreams and goals to be successful, but unfortunately this is not always the case. I'm not saying this to discourage you; quite the opposite, in fact: Once we overcome these challenges, we forever change the frequency at which we vibrate and become better creators of our own happiness.

This is very exciting and empowering and why I'm so passionate about working with Archangel

Nathaniel. He can take you to the next step in evolution and wake you up to a whole new existence—an existence filled with clarity, bravery, and the knowledge that nothing we desire is ever out of reach. All we need to master is how to work *with* the energy around us instead of working against it. Archangel Nathaniel is the powerful angel here to usher us into this new era of self-awareness so we can gain clarity about ourselves and what we truly want in life.

COMMUNICATION WITH NATHANIEL

Nathaniel's interaction with humanity is unique compared to other angels I have worked with, whose communication feels very external: You receive guidance and are aware that the angel you have called on is helping you. Nathaniel works in a very different way. If you are new to working with Nathaniel, you may not know that this powerful angel is even assisting you. Nathaniel works through you and with you.

This is powerful because you yourself begin feeling the changes you need to make in your life. This guidance does not feel like it's coming from an external source, it is simply you waking up to what no longer resonates in your life.

When we have stagnant energy present in our auras and lives, it drags us down and keeps us from realizing our true potential. Nathaniel works through us to wake us up to what no longer works. Being in Nathaniel's presence gives us a taste of what it feels like to be truly limitless. Excuses, obstacles, and problems all drop away. We feel energized and rejuvenated, with a renewed sense of purpose.

CLEARING AWAY THE OLD

In order to bring new energy into your life, you must first make room for it. Clearing away the old is what Archangel Nathaniel is best at. In order to manifest at our highest level we must match our energy to that which we desire. Financial abundance, love, and happiness all vibrate at similar frequencies. Many people have trouble, because the energy of what they desire is absent in their lives. Instead, they have lives filled with things that no longer resonate. The energy of stagnation and lack is heavy and low. Attempting to manifest high-frequency desires, such as happiness and love, is difficult when the energy around us does not match. Archangel Nathaniel helps us let go of old energy, allowing room for fresh new growth.

When I began working with Nathaniel, he guided me to let go of relationships that were not genuine. When I first started traveling the world to teach, I met a lot of people and formed some amazing friendships—but I also made a lot of connections that I could feel in my heart had much more to do with who my mother is than who *I* am. On the surface it never really bothered me that I could feel these aspects of some of my acquaintances—I never really thought about it, as I am actually quite used to it. However, having and maintaining these one-sided connections was actually hurting the energy of my life more than I realized.

When Nathaniel started working through me, it was as if my highest self, the most honest part of me, came to the surface. I will never forget lying on the floor one afternoon with my phone in my hand, deleting contact after contact, without giving it a second thought. Normally I would feel guilty doing something like this—I would consider it to be too negative, and instead I would just deal with the imbalance of the status quo. However, on this day I mustered no such excuses, and I wiped out a good portion of my contact list without hesitation.

What I had actually done didn't really set in until later that day, when I prayed I wouldn't be seen as rude or inconsiderate for metaphorically walking away from these people. Interestingly enough, as days passed, I realized I wasn't hearing from any of these people anymore—and this was before mobile phones had a block feature, so something else, something divine, was going on, and Nathaniel knew then what I eventually learned. By breaking these connections in my own mind and energy, I had actually completely severed them, and it was only later that I realized the benefit.

You see, up to that point in my teaching career, I had taught in four or five countries, but I was praying I would be invited to many more. And in the three months after doing something as seemingly innocuous as deleting a few contacts and connections, I was invited to three additional countries. To me, that was a real dream come true—and the invitations kept coming.

That situation taught me so much—but it also highlighted just how little we, as humans, ever really know about our manifestations at any given point. I realized how even the smallest imbalance can have a dramatic impact on our ability to attract our dreams and desires. When we let go of even seemingly small imbalances in our lives, we make room for potentially huge new opportunities!

Working with Nathaniel is an invaluable experience because from his vantage point he can see clearly the aspects of our lives that are out of balance. All we must do once we call on this powerful angel is to live our lives and follow the internal guidance that comes from the heightened sensitivity Nathaniel brings. Often people question why they are being led in a certain direction when they are following their guidance. Of course, this complicates any assistance the angels are attempting to provide. Because Archangel Nathaniel works *through* us, we question less. This fast-tracks our progress. When we are guided by Nathaniel, we don't overthink, hesitate, or doubt ourselves—we charge ahead following our guidance fearlessly. Focusing our energy and our intent in such a manner is a powerful way to manifest!

THE ARCHANGEL OF THE NEXT STEP

Archangel Nathaniel, whose name means "gift of God," has been working silently with humanity for a very long time. He has a red aura that relates to the fire of our passion, our dreams of happiness, and our hearts' desires.

Nathaniel is the angel that comes to you when you reach that point where you just *know* deep down that the time for positive change and forward movement is now. Whether you're manifesting a soul mate or the discovery of your life purpose, Nathaniel comes to you when you reach that moment where you think: *Okay, it's time—I've done everything I possibly can to prepare for and create this change. Now let's see it, universe!*

Nathaniel comes to us when we know that no other possibility for our future exists besides that which we have been praying for and working toward. Nathaniel then works through us to fine-tune our lives, to help us feel safe walking away from the parts of our lives, or the relationships in our lives, that are taking much more than they are returning. He helps us to be honest with ourselves so we no longer cling to the excuses of why we won't change what we know must be changed. It is then, and only then, that we are finally ready for our next step.

But being ready is what I want to talk with you about now . . .

THE ANGELIC AGENT OF CHANGE

When I say that Nathaniel is the angel of change, I mean it in the strongest and most literal sense. When you call upon Nathaniel to help you make necessary changes in your life, those changes *will* happen. It isn't as if Nathaniel is controlling you; instead, you start to become completely honest with yourself and you'll often find yourself saying, "No, this doesn't work for me anymore—good-bye."

It's as if blinders have been removed from the eyes of your heart and soul, allowing you to clearly see what does and does not work for you. You become much more aware of your own energy and less tolerant of any aspect of life that has a draining or imbalanced effect. This could relate to people, places, jobs, or your current life path—anything. So it's important to note that you must truly and completely be ready for change if you call upon Nathaniel. Be prepared for Nathaniel to work with you in such a way that you will no longer be able to repress or ignore the feeling that something, no matter what it is, no longer works for you.

All changes the angels guide us to make are positive—but that does not mean the change will always feel fun, easy, or consequence-free. We humans have a tendency to become complacent to even harmful situations: We form dependencies that are sometimes not in our best interests. We set out on paths that we keep going along, even if we are shown clear and repetitive signs that this isn't the best direction for us, because we already have put in so much effort that we do not want to acknowledge that we were wrong or have to start over. It is during these times and during the changes related to these situations that we need to keep the most faith.

Remember that with change of any level of magnitude comes a period of transition. And depending on how *much* change you're guided to make, the transition may feel more or less comfortable or unsettling. I'm sure you've heard the old adage that in order to let in the new, you must first let go of the old . . . well, Archangel Nathaniel is the personification of this wisdom.

So if you're in a relationship, job, city, friendship, or other situation that you know isn't working for you, but you're too afraid to make an immediate change because you fear there are no suitable alternatives, consider this fact before calling on Nathaniel. I can tell you that there are zero documented cases of Nathaniel's guidance causing anyone to ruin their lives or make sacrifices beyond what is reasonable—Nathaniel works very fast, and the divine replacement for what we let go of always seems to come exactly when we need it. Depending on how much or how little you've been listening to and following your guidance up to this point, your experience with this magnificent and powerful arch-angel will vary.

My experience with Nathaniel has been both confusing (when I find myself making changes I didn't know I needed to make) and rewarding. I would never tell anyone not to work with Nathaniel—but I feel it is only fair for me to include the caveat in the above paragraph so you're aware of the reality.

If you're at all like me, change is exciting. Especially when you're praying a lot and following the signs you're getting. Because, you know that if something leaves your life for any reason, it will be replaced with something else much more fitting. Nathaniel has taught me not to hold on to the now, and not to get too comfortable in any situation, as we often don't know what step we may next be guided to make toward a new purpose in life. Life is so complex and so involved that it is not always easy for us humans to consciously see what exactly needs to be changed. Nathaniel, however, teaches us that our higher selves always know what does and does not work for us—and the more time we spend connected to this ascended part of our being, the better decisions we make for ourselves and the more of our purpose we are allowed to experience in this lifetime.

Call upon Nathaniel when you feel that you have done everything else in your power to get to that next great step in life. Working with this angel will immediately get you in touch with your higher self so you can make necessary and important corrections to your course and daily life. Anytime working with Nathaniel starts to become overwhelming and you feel it would be easier to not be so aware of the changes you need to make, you can ask him to stop bringing this awareness to you. He will stop immediately—and trust me, there is no shame in doing this if you feel guided to. It can be very overwhelming to live life every day no longer able to ignore the issues and imbalances you face. So feel free to call on Nathaniel in spurts—a lot of people who work with him do exactly that. Once you have managed the current changes in your life, call on him again to help show you what must be changed next.

Please don't think this will transform your life into one giant housecleaning mission. Although angels like Nathaniel do guide us to actually make changes, our motivation to continue working through them always comes in the form of answered prayers. As I said before, when you let go of something, you make room for something new—and the more you experience this, the more you will continue to ask Nathaniel to reveal imbalance in your life so you can correct it and move on to a better tomorrow.

•————————————————•

Exercise: Calling Upon Nathaniel

With your energy centered, your heart and your mind open to the essence of your purpose, please just invoke Archangel Nathaniel's name in your mind. Feel the energy of this archangel's name, which means "gifts of God." Archangel Nathaniel's divine purpose is to turn the fires of our passion, the power of our desire, into the reality around us. As we call upon Archangel Nathaniel, we ask him to surround us in light. And love and hold us.

Say: "Archangel Nathaniel, as you come to be with me in this moment, I ask you to please begin looking deep into my heart. Looking past any walls that I've built—any pain that I hold on to—deep into the pure center of my being. I ask you to please see who I truly am. To see who I came here to be. Underneath everything that I've learned, everything that I've experienced in this body, I ask you to please connect with this purity, this essence of my being. To remember the divine truth. To see who and what I am.

"And I ask you, Nathaniel, to please begin to bring this energy to the surface. No longer will it be buried through pain, through hesitation, through doubt. Through what society has told me is or is not possible. And this moment, Nathaniel, I liberate this inner part of myself. I unleash my true self. And ask that this energy comes clearly to the surface. To be with me. And to remain with me. And to remind me in all situations what is right for me and what is no longer right for me.

"Archangel Nathaniel, I am ready to live my purpose now. I choose purpose. I choose happiness. And so I ask you to please work with me, to please work through me, so that every step that I take from this moment forward is a step on my path directly toward purpose.

Thank you, Archangel Nathaniel, and thank You, God."

Although Nathaniel works very fast, helping us to become aware of needed changes almost overnight, please do not think that heaven holds any expectations that we *make* those changes overnight.

If you ever feel stagnant or confused about which changes to make next, you can always call on Archangel Nathaniel. While Nathaniel is great at helping us rid ourselves of the fear of making changes, Archangel Michael, whom we will work with in the next chapter, is the angel to call upon to dispel the fear of actually moving forward once the blocks are removed.

It's one thing to have an opportunity presented to you—it's entirely another to know if that opportunity is the right one for you. It's important to work to get past our fears, especially the FOMO (fear of missing out) that sometimes causes us to go down a path that isn't exactly right for us. Working daily with Archangel Michael can help us to release fear so we always remember who we are and why we came here, and remind us to never compromise on our path. We are never meant to accept less than exactly what our heart guides us toward.

Chapter 7

DISPELLING FEARS WITH ARCHANGEL MICHAEL

Archangel Michael's name means "He who is like God," and just like God, Michael is omnipresent (everywhere). He is the angelic equivalent of a superhero who can come to everyone's assistance simultaneously.

Michael knows what your life purpose is, so you can call upon him for direction about the best career that will be meaningful. Michael also provides courage, confidence, and protection. Three ways to know that Michael is with you are:

- A feeling of warm energy
- Feeling relaxed and safe

- Seeing sparkles of light blue and purple lights (with no health or eye issues that would lead to lights in the visual field)

Archangel Michael helps people to feel confident and driven as they witness and take part in the changes happening around them.

Since so many of us live somewhat solitary spiritual home lives, Archangel Michael's lessons will be key to helping us find and maintain the confidence to know that our path toward purpose is, in fact, the correct path.

OVERCOMING FEARS OF DREAMS FULFILLED

Why is it that we humans always consider happiness to be fleeting and temporary? Why is it that "too good to be true" is such a popular phrase? We perpetuate these beliefs because we don't feel we have seen enough evidence to the contrary in life. Our fear of failure and ridicule is enough to transform the way we think, pray, and hope. While we all have our wants, we often keep them categorized in order of what we consider to be most to least achievable, as discussed in Part I.

Why is it that we are so drawn toward happiness but simultaneously so afraid of it? Have you ever asked yourself why exactly you have entertained thoughts of not being able to reach your goals or achieve your dreams? I have seen cases of fear so ingrained that people will literally laugh at their own dreams and instantly shut down to any possibility of having a happier life. Archangel Michael wants to help us get past this mentality.

I'm sure you've heard the saying "There is nothing to fear but fear itself"—and we all know how clichéd it has become over the years, but there's actually a lot we can learn from those words. We are energy, our souls are energy, and our thoughts are also energy. We, as beings, vibrate with certain frequencies depending on the state of our minds, bodies, and souls.

The energy of fear is what I consider to be an absolute lack of positive forward progress. Fear is a dense energy and vibration, and our souls have relatively limited space. This means that at any given point, our souls only have so much room for vibrational energy—so if we hold on to lower energy, *it* becomes our vibration.

I know fear is normal; I know certain fears are essential for survival. The fear we are discussing is not about survival—it is the lingering and, if you think about it, often illogical and ill-founded sensation that making positive change is risky. Because fear has always played such an essential role in life, it's very difficult to know when or even how to separate yourself from the harmful forms of it. I mean, if you're manifesting a new job in a new city, but the reality of that move is that you could fail and lose everything, who in their right mind would tell you not to be afraid?

Archangel Michael would, and for good reason.

When it is the divine time to take action, you'll know. One of the best ways to know that you *really* know is to try ignoring the guidance. If you ignore divine guidance when the time to take action is now, I can assure you that you won't find peace until you follow it.

Trust me, I've been there. It's easy to feel the comfort in avoiding your fears—but it's near impossible to find long-term peace in ignoring your guidance. Even if you still have logical fears, you'll eventually find yourself so detached from whatever your fear is trying to get you to hold on to that one day it will almost be as if you step outside yourself as you witness yourself finally following your guidance. It will just *happen*.

Because heaven knows us so well, the time to start on that new path will always be undeniable. If it's easy for you to deny, then you can trust that it isn't the right moment to take action yet.

Pretty easy when you think about it that way, isn't it? It's *supposed* to be that easy. Sure, we may get impatient waiting for the moment of pure clarity—but it will come, and when it does, it's undeniable.

CONFIDENCE FROM ARCHANGEL MICHAEL

Archangel Michael is amazing at helping us to expedite our manifestations, because a lot of time that we spend waiting for divine guidance is really just a period to release our fears. However, Michael doesn't just release fear—he also instills a powerful knowing and confidence in us.

Heaven and the angels know that following your true guidance (the kind that doesn't change or go away with time) will always lead to a great outcome. Their goal is to help us learn this same truth—whatever it takes. When you feel fear, you can be sure that it is a sign to pray, and to call upon Michael.

This powerful archangel is not only great at allowing us to feel more confident, but Michael is also an amazing planner. When we take the very important step of asking Archangel Michael to help us to release our fears, not only do we immediately gain access to his majestic level of confidence—but we also start to see through the situation.

Fear has such powerful energy that it becomes self-sustaining within our souls. When we allow fear to remain in our consciousness, it blocks our ability to see around it. So while we may search our minds (or the Internet) for solutions and safety nets to get past our fear, it is blocking us from seeing what we actually need to know to get rid of it. It can become a constant loop of having fear, trying to think of ways around it, and ending up right back in fear.

This is why working with Archangel Michael is essential—he helps to release us from harmful thought and decision-making patterns. Michael has a way of immediately releasing the burden of concern when we call upon him—and it is during these unburdened times that we should be thinking about our manifestations.

We take so many unnecessary and often self-sabotaging steps to protect ourselves when we set forth on a new path, but with prayer we can save ourselves a lot of trouble, and actually make this transition a joyous one—because it should be. Try it next time you feel yourself consumed with fears and concerns.

Exercise:
Fear Release with
Archangel Michael

Take deep breaths as you feel guided, and with each exhale just picture yourself becoming lighter and lighter—and allow yourself to actually feel the fear leaving your body and aura. After you've given yourself permission to exist in this peaceful state for a few minutes, begin to visualize yourself in the situation you are planning or hoping for. Anytime you feel fear creeping back in, just take another breath in . . . ask Michael to release it . . . and exhale the fear away.

Keep doing this. The more you do, the easier it is to maintain a peaceful state. Keep seeing yourself or your life in direct contact with your dreams and manifestations. Stay there, move around in this visualization, and keep breathing out the fear.

This really should be a daily exercise for you; this is such a powerful way to get connected with your path and purpose. Call upon Michael using whatever words come naturally to you (remember there is no ritual to working with the angels) and ask that your fear be released.

Here is an example of what you might say:

"Dear Archangel Michael, I ask you to please come be with me and to surround me with your energy. I ask you to please allow your heavenly vibration to surround and uplift my soul—please begin to infuse me with your strength. In this moment, Michael, I ask you to please help me to release my fear permanently and I ask you to please help me honestly process any related emotions so I can move on and never have to relive this block again. I affirm to God, heaven, and the angels that from this moment forward I will no longer sit idly by as fear exists in my soul—I will work with Archangel Michael to process and release any and all lower energy that does not serve me and no longer has a lesson for me to learn."

DISCOVERING YOUR PATH

Archangel Michael not only helps us to move forward on our chosen path, but he is adept at helping us sort through our thoughts to discover our path and purpose in the first place. It's really easy for humans to become totally lost in modern society. Expectations are imposed upon us, and we often go down certain paths just because the opportunity was there. It's all too common that we find our lives so far afield from where we want to be—where we are supposed to be—that making our way back to our divine place seems impossible.

As I always say, your soul knows what you are supposed to be doing. Oftentimes, even those who feel the most lost have an idea of what direction is right for them. It can be so overwhelming, though, to sort through all of the possible things a human could do on this planet and decide on the exact one you're mean for. Especially if you're like me and you enjoy doing many different things, those can't all be our purpose, right?

Purpose will never mean one thing—it will never point to one specific time in your life—it will always be the journey and everything you are guided to do along it. For some people, purpose is one thing; for others, it is a constantly evolving set of things that may or may not seem to have anything to do with each other.

If you want clarity and you're having trouble finding it on your own, you should ask Michael for it. If you remember that one of the best ways to identify true heavenly guidance is to look for consistency in the messages and guidance that come to you, that's really all you need to know to eventually find your path. Stop spending time in your head alone, trying to identify where or with whom you should go . . . and start asking for clarity every day, several times a day.

After you ask Archangel Michael for help, the next important step is to let go as much as you can. When you hold on to, or try to force, the outcome of a prayer, you can block the answer. Heaven works best in a relationship of mutual trust. When you trust enough to let go of what you're asking and praying about, heaven has an opportunity to give you *reasons* to trust. From that point you'll actually be very pleasantly surprised by how rapid and clear your guidance is.

Heaven does sometimes work on a timing scale that differs from what we prefer—but we can always trust that when we do receive messages of clarity, it is exactly when we were supposed to receive them. That only serves to release any more fear we may have, and to show us that heaven has done an incredible job of guiding us through the powerful and confidence-inspiring energy of Michael.

We've talked a lot about fears and blocks related to our own life experience and thought process—but did you know that there are many blocks we humans encounter that actually transcend our current lives? There are issues, fears, and energy related to our past lives as well.

While it's relatively easy to make a list of the issues we need to heal from in this lifetime, what if your biggest block relates to pain or disappointment you picked up a few lifetimes ago but have never been able to clear? In the next chapter, we are going to talk about and work with karmic and past-life influences on our current path.

Chapter 8

CLEARING THE OFTEN UNSEEN: KARMA AND CORDS

Among the many factors we weigh when self-determining our eligibility for happiness, our interpretation of where we stand karmically is far too often taken into consideration. As you likely know, karma is the universal force that states simply, "what goes around, comes around."

Karma is an incredible force of balance in the universe that ensures all living beings ultimately share the same amount of life experience over the course of our existence. Throughout all of our lifetimes, each of us will have experienced the exact same amount of everything. We will all have riches; we will all have been poor . . . and everything in between. We will all live lives as every gender and sexuality. We will all feel powerful; we will all feel weak. We will all have lived long lives, and we will all have gone before our perceived time.

There is a need for complete balance with respect to all aspects of energy, and our human existence is no exception. This is another reason why we should *never* feel guilty for allowing blessings into our lives.

KARMA AND MANIFESTATION

Even if people around you do not seem to have the same access to blessings as you do, this does not mean you are somehow less eligible for them. The blessings heaven sends us are meant to empower us to continue to spread this energy. The more abundant you are, in any way, the more you can help others. The more you help others, the happier you will be, and, therefore, the more blessings you will attract. Karma is something we should all be aware of, but it is not something we should ever assume we fully understand.

As long as we think we understand the massive complexities of karma, we may preemptively try to do karma's work through our own manifestations.

We make assumptions (either consciously or subconsciously) about where we stand in relation to our own karma. What I mean by this is that there are those who believe so strongly in karma that they assume they know exactly what they do and do not deserve as a result of their actions in life, or what has happened to them. We assume that as a result of our or other people's actions, there is now a definitive imbalance that must be corrected.

What we don't always grasp about karma is just how long it has been a part of the human soul's journey—and how it spans lifetimes. If you did something at any point that caused someone else physical or emotional pain, the normal assumption is that you now have bad karma. What we don't take into consideration, because of how difficult and complex it would be to decipher, is the possibility that we have lived prior lives with the soul of that person in different roles. There *are* times when doing something bad to someone creates a karmic imbalance—yet an equal number of times, those actions serve to actually balance a karmic agreement. This doesn't mean we should all behave like sociopaths and do whatever we want—but it definitely means that we are too powerful to make assumptions either way.

The second you decide you're not worthy of something, you start to make it true. So I find that the healthiest relationship to have with karma is a purely passive one. How can you know for sure why a situation had the outcome it did? Maybe you did something really nice for someone. Can you honestly say for a fact that you now have good karma as a result? How do you know they didn't do something equivalent or greater for you in a past life? How can you know if they didn't do something great for someone else, and you're just the instrument of their good karma in return?

Can we ever say with certainty that we know when and where a karmic connection originated?

When we find ourselves in a situation where we have an effect on another person, or vice versa, it is impossible to know in that moment just what karmic aspects are at play. Since karma crosses lifetimes, your biggest regret in life may have been meant to be, on a karmic level. It is unfair to ever assume that we deserve more or less in life because of our actions—good or bad.

We should always assume we deserve the greatest amount of happiness we can find in life. Even if we do good deeds for others, we should never feel entitled to blessings in return. All that does is create expectation in our minds, and if those expectations do not align with what we are divinely meant to experience, it can lead to disappointment. And when we live in disappointment or any other lower energy, of course it affects our mood, prayers, and outlook on life.

I put this chapter in this book not to scare you or cause you to overthink karma. I am writing about it because I want to encourage you to let go of your assumptions. Whether you *think* you have accrued good or bad karma along the way, your thoughts cannot impact *karma* in any fashion—all they can do is interfere with your life path and *manifestations*.

I find that doing good things for other people, with no need for reward—not even a karmic one—is the most enlightened mentality to maintain. When you do something good for someone, do it because you believe good things should happen in this world. Trust that happiness is something we are all entitled to, no matter what.

I am a giver, so I know just how good it feels to see someone smile when I am able to help them in any way. I find that attaching karmic expectations or assumptions to my deeds only cheapens them and detracts from the situation. If I am guided to do something good for someone, I can safely assume that they are divinely meant to experience it—and I am the means heaven has chosen to deliver it. Nothing could feel better than that.

I take these situations as clear signs that I am on the right path in life, considering them gifts and karmic rewards in and of themselves because, if you're like me, not much feels better than helping someone find happiness on this planet. And it certainly brings me joy to know that I am on the right path.

UNDERSTANDING CORDS

Throughout our lifetimes and in every situation our soul experiences, we form energetic connections. These connections come in all forms you can imagine, such as connections of love, friendship, fondness, convenience . . . and on the lower end of the spectrum, resentment, fear, hate, and even codependence. These connections help us to form a relationship with the world around us and serve to keep what works for us close—and allows the situations that do not work for us to become opportunities to heal and learn. These connections happen automatically as a passive result of the dynamic of the situation you are in. As a living being, you inevitably form these energetic connections with the world around you—and while most connections have obvious roles, there are some connections that are more balanced than others.

Cords represent connections of imbalance. Cords got their name from the way they are seen energetically—they appear almost as an etheric surgical tubing of sorts that transfers energy instead of life-sustaining fluids.

Before I get too far into the description and explanation of cords, I want to talk about the aspect of our souls that causes cords to arise in the first place. You see, our souls are constantly growing and evolving—and while our brains process the material and emotional aspects of the situations we encounter, our souls will always see and experience the spiritual truth of each situation. This is why it isn't uncommon to get gut feelings, sometimes when no logic backs them up—we just *know*. While each of us is connected to the energy of our souls with different levels of sensitivity—our souls are constantly having conversations with the world around us.

When you are in a healthy situation, there is an even give-and-take from the souls involved. When you have as much to offer as you receive, there is balance and the connections in that environment are safe. The second a situation starts to take more from you than it offers, an energetic imbalance occurs.

When you meet someone new who seems very friendly, for example, you may find that you feel drawn to them—but later on, after you've had some time to yourself, you realize you want nothing to do with them. Your soul probably had some observations about that encounter that your brain missed. Now that your mind and your soul are in sync, the truth of your opinion can come to the surface. Underneath it all, they really just wanted something from you or were using you to gain something, and a cord formed.

Our souls want to live in energetic balance, but whenever we feel that something outside us is responsible for disruption of any form *inside* us, we send out cords. Cords are a transfer of energy; when we want or expect something from an outside source and do not receive it, we still find a way to get something else. In the case of cords, we get balance, or at least the illusion of it.

You see, our souls are meant to be self-sustaining. Ultimately, in human evolution, we will all ascend to a state where we no longer harbor expectations of others, where we no longer require anything outside ourselves to find true peace and happiness. This is why self-actualized people like Mother Teresa, Nelson Mandela, and Mahatma Gandhi are so admired—our souls could see how humanity is supposed to be through their actions.

Believe it or not, though, cords can teach us a lot and actually serve as amazing forms of guidance. If I'm upset about something, that means I had expectations. When my expectations are not met, and as a result I get upset, there is a disruption in my soul's energy. This disruption, like all energy, wants to balance itself out. Since my mind is focused on what caused the disruption, I create an energetic connection to that person or situation. Once that cord is formed, my soul's energy gets the illusion of balance.

Our expectations are actually energetic voids inside us, and cords serve to fill those voids. I like to think of cords as energetic pacifiers, because the truth is, if our happiness is contingent on the actions of others, we are missing something inside ourselves: personal growth and peace. Since personal growth, inner peace, and enlightenment cannot be faked, our cords tell us the truth about ourselves.

Whenever we make the conscious decision that we are upset because of anything outside ourselves, we are sending out cords. When a cord is formed, it allows us to find a sort of resolution with the situation, because even though we are upset, at least we know *why* we are upset, and that is often enough for us. What we should be doing when we get upset is asking ourselves, *What is it about me that needs to grow in order for this to no longer upset me?* A lot of yogis think like that; some even go out of their way to upset their students so they are forced to look within and discover why they reacted that way.

Our mission on this planet is to evolve on a soul level—and cords, believe it or not, can actually help us, because they serve as clear evidence of what part of ourselves we need to work on. When we give ourselves the illusion that it is okay to be upset and remain upset about something, the resulting cords actually attach us to those situations.

Cords are the representation of current imbalance. Cords can follow us from lifetime to lifetime if we do not release them, trapping us in a situation or a pattern if we aren't aware of their energy. The good news about cords is that they are easy to cut. The angels are very enthusiastic about helping us release connections to energy that no longer serves us. I personally feel that cord cutting should be an everyday exercise, and it doesn't have to complicate your existing daily routine.

We have a lot more control over the energy that is allowed to influence us than we think. It's very easy to feel like a victim of lower energy, especially when it seems powerful or inescapable. This is another major way cords can help us—because they are so easy to release, we get an opportunity to actually experience how powerful we are.

It doesn't matter if you're sending or receiving the cords—it doesn't matter if they came from this lifetime or past lives—if imbalance exists, heaven wants to help you clear and heal from it. Just like every other aspect of working with heaven, there is no ritual—but if you're unfamiliar with working on your cords and want to know a great way to get started, please follow along.

Exercise: Cord Cutting

I find that all energetic work is best done in a relaxed state. You can do this exercise while you're stressed or full of other potentially distracting energy—but the more relaxed you are, the easier it is to let go.

Start off by taking a few deep breaths. If you have access to soft music and feel it will help you relax, please play some. Position yourself in a comfortable way—sitting, lying, or standing; it doesn't matter—and continue breathing.

As you start to feel yourself de-stress and feel more peaceful, ask the angels to come be with you. You don't have to call them by name if it doesn't come naturally to you—the angels you need in any given moment know, and will always come to help when you ask, regardless of formalities.

Ask the angels to scan your body entirely— looking for any connections of imbalance from this lifetime or past lifetimes. Ask the angels to begin working with you and through you to help you to release these connections: "Angels, please remove any and all energetic connections that no longer serve me."

Take another deep breath and feel yourself becoming lighter.

It's really that easy. Most people who experience this for the first time are surprised by how much energy they are able to release. Don't be shocked if old memories, or even past-life memories, pop into your mind. There will never be a need to know the origin of a cord, but cords do carry specific energy, so if you feel yourself revisiting an old pain, just keep breathing and ask the angels to help you process and release these emotions. If it ever feels like it's too much to handle, you can stop anytime you like. All that matters is that you do as much as you can, when you can.

●————————————————————●

BREAKING PATTERNS

It is difficult to explain to anyone how it feels to have cords. We are often born with them, and we progressively take them on and send them out throughout our current lifetime, so we become acclimated to their vibration. Cords feel like heaviness; they bring about an energy of not being able to let go of situations—you always know if you have cords if certain thoughts keep you from being able to fall asleep. When you cut cords, you'll likely feel lighter, happier, and all around have a better sense of well-being— you'll definitely sleep better! Anytime a certain type of person or situation seems to be a repetitive fixture in your life, regardless of how hard you try to avoid it, you can be sure there are cords involved.

If you keep experiencing heartbreak, money issues, random injuries, or any other undesirable pattern, it's very likely that you have an energetic connection to those situations on a soul level—and it's time to sever those connections. It is common for people with love and money issues to have cords attached to past lives involving vows of chastity or poverty that they never broke. Discovering this can help many people who otherwise could have spent several *more* lifetimes trying to break those patterns.

Ask the angels if *you* have any vows from past lives that are negatively impacting your current life. If you feel like you might, then please ask the angels to immediately cut those cords, and say an affirmative prayer stating that you hereby release this old energy immediately and permanently.

Prayer to Help with Love

"Dear God and angels, I ask you to please look deep into my heart, to see the truth of my soul. I ask you to please see any and all energy around my heart—any walls I have built, and blocks or pain I hold on to. I ask you to please see how this life, as well as my past lives, has had an effect on my ability and willingness to allow in love. In this moment I affirm to you that I am ready to begin healing from my pain and I am ready to let down my guard.

"Angels, I ask you to please help me to feel safe allowing love into my life—and I ask you to please help me feel confident enough to send love. From this moment forward I ask you to please work with me in every aspect of my existence to guide my actions to align myself once again with the vibration of love. I forgive the past, I accept the divinity of what has happened, and I let go of resentment. I feel myself opening up completely to the divinity of what and who may lie before me on my path.

"I choose love for this lifetime, and I hereby denounce any vows I made in past lives that

would keep me from feeling the closeness of love. In this moment I ask you, heaven, to please align my life with the vibration of love so that I can once again welcome this energy into my life completely and permanently."

LIFTING THE ENERGY

When a cord is cut, healing begins—no matter if you were sending or receiving that cord. Cords are called energetic pacifiers because as long as a cord is present in a situation, the imbalance does not heal itself. Cords do come back after you've cut them; they are a consequence of an energetic dynamic, not the cause. So anytime an aspect of imbalance is still current in your life, the cord will re-form. If you have disagreements or tension at work, and you cut your cords at home—unless you think about or reenter that situation, the cord will usually stay away. However, the second the energy of that imbalance becomes current, the cord will once again be present.

What is great about this is that the more we cut our cords, the more we acclimate to living *without* them. Cords tend to drain our energy—they make us feel heavy and tired. The more we cut them, the more of our own soul energy we regain access to— our resonant life force is more present, and we simply start to feel better in almost every regard.

Cutting cords improves sleep, energy levels, mental function, memory . . . in short, it gives you back your spark. With enough time, you begin to consider this new energy to be normal, because it *is*, and you become highly sensitive to cords when you pick them up.

Cords instantly disrupt our energy fields, and those who cut theirs regularly know the sensation. This can serve as a very powerful barometer for energetic balance in life. When you work regularly with your cords, you'll find that your intuition about people, situations, and opportunities is remarkably enhanced, which will only serve your decision making as you move forward on your life path toward purpose.

I find that using the seemingly inevitable low energy in our world to guide and aid our path will always be the healthiest relationship we can have with it. If you spend your time trying to avoid cords and other lower energy, you may not learn the lessons they have for us.

We are incredibly powerful beings. All humans have the ability to exercise complete control over the energy we allow to influence our lives—but we have been taught to the contrary.

The more time you spend being conscious of and working on your own energy, the more you will learn about your own power. I am a firm believer that the more time you allow yourself to spend in balanced and higher energy, the more you start to consider it normal. You'll become even more sensitive, and it won't be long before you replace the question "How can I avoid lower energy?" with "I refuse to experience lower energy."

Of all of the lower energy, imbalanced connections, blocks, and fears we potentially encounter from lifetime to lifetime, it's important to remember that we are ultimately in control of the energy we allow to linger in our lives. As we work to clear and permanently release our blocks and fears, it's very important to work to heal ourselves on both an emotional and a spiritual level to ensure we have completely moved on from these blocks.

Archangel Raphael, as we will learn in the next chapter, is *the* angel to call upon for all things healing related. As you go through that chapter remember that healing is something that should take place at a pace you feel comfortable with and is a process that should never be rushed. Move forward and heal at the pace that feels natural for you, and you'll feel the loving energy of Archangel Raphael guiding and comforting you each step of the journey.

Chapter 9

HEALING FROM PAST PAIN WITH ARCHANGEL RAPHAEL

If you find that dreaming of your desires brings you anxiety, frustration, pain, fear, or doubt, congratulations—these feelings relate to exactly what blocks are in your way.

While at first it may not seem like a good thing to connect with these lower emotions, learning about what you need to heal from is key to progress. While we are never meant to dwell in negativity, if you find that certain emotions keep coming to the surface, you can take that as a clear sign that it is time to process and release this energy.

When you manifest, you have to want it with every aspect of your mind, body, and soul. The clearer you are energetically and emotionally, the easier it is to maintain positive thoughts and prayer.

Our experiences come to make up who we are as we move through our lifetimes, and ultimately—the entirety of our soul.

GETTING BACK ON THE SOUL'S PATH

Archangel Raphael, who is known as the healing angel and the angel of healers, works with each and every one of us in our pursuit of happiness and purpose. The angels know very well how much emotional and physical pain affects every aspect of our lives, and Raphael is the main archangel working with us to heal from all of this.

Every ounce of energy we experience and retain within ourselves, both high and low, affects the way we make decisions. When we hold on to emotional trauma and pain from the past, there is a certain amount of acceptance that goes into that retention. We may harbor excuses as to why we hold on to this energy, such as: "It wasn't my fault," "I'm not ready to let go," or, most commonly, "I don't know *how* to let go of my pain." However, the fact remains that as long as we allow pain, resentment, unforgiveness, or anger to stay within us, it remains a part of us, and the situations that caused those emotions never really end.

In relationships, for example, it is very common for heartbreak to cause people to want to spend a lot of time alone—or jump right into a new relationship before they have time to process and heal from the old one. Either way, the pain of the past caused the person to make a decision that was not consonant with their soul's desire or guidance. We often make decisions in life that have nothing to do with what our hearts really want; instead, we make them based on what we feel will keep us safe from having to experience more pain.

The logical mind may rationalize this sort of behavior. Yet you have to realize that when enough time goes by—and enough decisions based on hiding from pain are made—it isn't altogether uncommon to find you have deviated so far from your soul's path that you may have no idea how to even start the journey back to true happiness.

This is why *healing* is the topic of the final chapter in this book—without it, we are at the mercy of the tides our egos create, and that has never led anyone to lasting happiness, as the ego just wants to play it safe. There is a big difference between being happy and feeling the relief of knowing you're in a "safe" situation. We often confuse those two feelings—and this causes us a lot of confusion in life.

Say you're in a relationship with someone who really excites you. Everything about being with this person feels great, and you think it's really cute how they laugh. Their laugh is unique and attention getting—you're charmed by it.

Time goes by and the novelty of the relationship wanes—and as humans do, you become conditioned and accustomed to the behavior of the person you're spending time around. Everything seems to be going great until one day you see that person kissing someone else out on the street.

Heartbreak. *How could they do this to me?* The relationship ends.

More time goes by, and you finally feel ready to get back out there. So you set your radar for a person to whom you may feel an attraction, and one day you meet someone who fits that bill.

As you talk, you notice an eerily familiar quality about them—and it's their *laugh*. Suddenly you find yourself flooded with emotional memories of your previous relationship, and you can feel yourself losing interest in this person. Ultimately, you decide not to pursue anything, and you move on.

Ahh, that feels good, doesn't it? I mean, who would want an everyday reminder of the person who betrayed them? Good riddance.

Well, while that may seem like a reasonable outcome, let's explore this situation a bit and see exactly how not healing from our past can change our lives in sometimes dramatic ways.

I know critiquing someone's laugh isn't fair; it was meant to be a lighthearted example. You can replace it with another pet peeve: being a smoker, liking different music than you, loud snoring—whatever. Over time and as this list of deal breakers grows, we find ourselves filtering out so much (and for seemingly logical reasons) that we may not realize just how isolated we have become.

I can't count how many first-date stories I've heard where the conversation turns to what each person doesn't like in a partner and how they feel such relief and such a strong connection when they realize that they dislike the same things. The ego has a way of tricking us into believing that sharing dislikes means we are more compatible with a person. And while there is an argument to be made for why disliking undesirable traits is a good thing, my point is that we sometimes take this too far and become lost in our fears.

What the angels would like us to regularly do instead, not only on dates but in all aspects of our lives, is to focus more on the positive and the joy and excitement of what we are praying for.

HEALING PAIN-BASED BLOCKS

If you can relate to the preceding scenario, I'm sure you'll see that you, too, are limiting yourself in various ways because of your fear of repeating painful aspects of the past. This doesn't mean that you must now review your lives, past and present, in their entirety and pinpoint and possibly relive those painful moments. The solution to these pain-based blocks is actually very simple.

Call on Archangel Raphael and *ask* to be healed from any pain that is causing you to make fear-based decisions. As with all the angels, the second you call on Raphael, he immediately goes to work.

Healing from pain is often seen as a long, arduous, and unpleasant process that most would rather put off as long as possible. When we work with heaven, though, we find that the exact opposite is true.

You'd be surprised how much healing you can do without even realizing it. We hold on to so much that we don't need to, just because either we aren't aware we are holding on to it or we assume that it won't be easy to let go of. Angels are constantly guiding us to heal. My spiritually minded friends and I always laugh at how often, during a normal day in our lives, the angels will guide us to suddenly remember a painful or irritating situation from the past. And we always know this recollection is divinely guided if we can still feel the power of the emotions from the situation as we process it. If this ever happens to you, know that it is a sign that you are ready to finally let go of that situation.

Exercise: Releasing Past Pain with Archangel Raphael

The first thing you should do is call on the angels to help you and shield you by asking them either out loud or in your mind, *"Angels, I ask you to please come be with me and to work with me and protect me in this moment."*

There is no need to completely relive these moments, as I've said, but if you do experience any pain or low energy from these memories, it is very important that you not stuff it down or repress it. Know that the more you allow yourself to feel and process this pain in the presence of the angels, the less you'll be holding on to and the less you'll ever have to experience from that situation again. Simply put, Raphael's healing power *works* and you'll find yourself feeling the relief of expressing your emotions a lot sooner than you may expect. It's never fun to do this, but when you realize the benefit of finally letting go, you'll be like me and you'll rack your brain to get all the old junk out so you can experience higher and higher levels of energy in life.

Try saying this:

"Archangel Raphael, I ask you to please come into my life and work with me. I ask you to please see me as I exist here in this moment and to please scan my body and soul. I ask you to please become aware of any pain from the past that I am holding on to—and I ask you to please begin working with me to clear it, as I am divinely meant to do. Please be with me as I process these emotions and please embrace me, reminding me that I am not alone. Raphael, I ask you to please stay with me throughout my

Healing from Past Pain with Archangel Raphael

daily life and work with me to constantly heal from the heavy and painful past.

"Thank you, heaven and angels, for helping to take this pain away as I honestly process these emotions for the last time. I thank you for being with me and giving me comfort as I allow the past to stay in the past, and as I allow my newly healed energy to guide me to my blissful future."

● ———————————————————— ●

EXPRESS—DON'T REPRESS— YOUR EMOTIONS

We humans have an amazing way of convincing ourselves that if we swallow the pain, we no longer feel it or are affected by it. This, of course, is completely false. The key to healing is honesty. Being honest with yourself about exactly how you feel about a memory is the best way to release the pain of it. Many healers and lightworkers refuse to ever do so because they assume that since they work with angels, they are under an obligation to act like angels. They fail to process these strong negative

155

emotions from the past because it feels so good to be in the light and love of heaven. And I understand. We all do this.

Know this: Heaven will never expect a human to act like an angel. We are not obligated to smile 24-7 or to always be happy. Obviously, angel work brings a lot of happiness, but the key to moving forward to a better tomorrow is to let go of any weight from the past you're holding on to. We are allowed to be emotional; we are allowed to get angry. Only the ego would believe that once we open up to work with the angels, we are no longer allowed to experience human emotions. We are humans, and heaven expects us to *act* like humans

So if you feel pain, *please* express it—you can always ask the angels to help you do so in a constructive and healing manner. Unexpressed emotions do not vanish with time; they do not get easier to handle tomorrow—they stay within us in a timeless state and have a profound effect on our all-around spiritual and energetic being. It could be said that getting angry is the *most* spiritual thing you can do, if it's how you honestly feel.

PAST-LIFE ISSUES

Not all pain or fear we experience actually comes from this lifetime. As I discussed in the previous chapter, we carry emotions and connections throughout our lives if we haven't let them go. I've seen many scenarios where this has caused a great deal of pain in current lives.

A lady in her fifties or sixties wanted a reading with me because she was having chronic relationship issues. She told me that every single relationship she got involved in fell apart—often without warning—and she was sick of it. She just wanted to find love, and keep it.

I asked the angels if they had any messages for her regarding love in her life, and I was immediately shown a very clear message that she had lost her husband. I saw and felt that he had passed away, and the pain she held on to as a result was what was causing her relationship issues.

So I told her all about what the angels had shown me, and she said, "Charles, I've never been married, and to my knowledge none of my exes have passed away."

This sort of thing is normal in angel readings. If your client doesn't understand the message, it simply means the reading is not over yet. So I asked the angels for clarity. I asked them to show me why they offered that message and what it meant.

Again, they gave me the exact same message. When angels' messages are repetitive, you know they are accurate and real, so I definitely had to get to the bottom of this. I asked them, *when* did her husband die?—and they showed me it was in the 1920s.

There we go—it was a past life. When I told the woman that he had passed away in a previous life, I could tell this really didn't mean much to her, so I asked the angels how I could help her heal. They told me to ask her a few questions:

I inquired, "Have you been the one ending all of these relationships?"

"Yes," she answered.

"Do you feel that none of your partners were good enough for you?"

Again, she said yes.

"That's it, then," I replied. "When your husband died in your past life, I could see clearly how betrayed you felt—you were angry at him, and you never forgave him." I could also see clearly that she never remarried in that lifetime, so when she came into this life, she still had all of those emotions weighing on her soul.

So every time she began to feel closeness or love in this lifetime, she was instantly reconnected with the pain from her past life, and that caused her to reject her partner because she attributed these emotions to him. Who could blame her? Very few of us have clear memories of our past lives that we can connect to issues we have in our current lives.

When I explained all of this to her, she began to cry. It at last seemed to make sense to her. I asked her if she was willing to begin working to let go of this pain.

She said she was, so we called upon Archangel Raphael and asked him to please help her to process, and permanently release, the pain she felt and the connection she maintained to this situation.

I could hear in her voice and feel in her energy that Raphael helped her. I'm also positive that it helped her former husband in his new life, as well. I have met countless people who carry guilt from the pain they caused others in their past lives. This, too, causes us to modify and often limit how much happiness we allow into our lives because of the burden we carry in our souls. When we pray for less, we get less.

Not everyone will always have the luxury of knowing that a part of their current life is as a result of pain from a past life—so I find it very beneficial to assume some aspects from your past life *are* present, just to cover all bases.

When I invoke Raphael, I always ask that any pain from this lifetime, or past lifetimes, be released so I may be free of this lower energy. You'd be surprised how many phobias, pet peeves, and strong opinions come from past lives—and Archangel Raphael is willing and able to help us heal from and release anything that is causing us to limit ourselves or block our openness to happiness.

FEARLESS MANIFESTING

Our souls are fearless. Because they can always see through situations to the true dynamic within, our souls do not like to hold on to conditions. The more pain we release from the past, the more we get in touch with our souls' guidance. The more in touch with our souls we are, the easier it is for us to get in touch with our hearts' true desires. The more we manifest and pray from the heart, the happier we are with the outcome.

When we work with angels to manifest happiness, we are working toward true and lasting happiness. This can only come when we completely let go of the pain within us. Raphael makes this process easy and permanent. I don't know about you, but I am very happy to leave the past in the past—and especially in situations where another person caused me great pain, I am very happy to completely release any and all connections to that person and the situation.

The freedom we feel from healing and the way our minds are suddenly more open to manifesting amazing things for ourselves is astounding. There is no need to be afraid of the pain from our past, and there is no need to attempt healing without the loving companionship of the angels.

Now that we have put so much incredible effort into clearing our energy and our energetic connections, it's time to start moving forward on our life path with our incredible power of prayer, visualization, and positive affirmation. As you know now, what we allow ourselves to feel and see most consistently for our lives *is* what we attract.

So affirm that your life purpose is made manifest, with heaven and the angels guiding your steps, and know that the power to fulfill your dreams is within you, now and always!

AFTERWORD

Spreading Joy

Sure, you can change your own life, but how can you change the world? In order for you to understand world change, you have to realize just how integral to this planet you actually are. What you think about your life and about the state of your surroundings *matters.* If you are unhappy, the world is measurably less happy . . . if you are happy, the same rules apply!

A lot of us decide against doing anything to improve the world because we are so intimidated by the perceived enormity of the task. Instead, we focus on outward solutions like politics, hoping our leaders will light the flames of peace and they will spread throughout our planet. We can no longer live that way; it simply doesn't work.

Believing in yourself is essential not only to your own personal goals, but also to heaven's goal of bringing peace to our planet. The more you tell yourself that you matter (because you *do*!), the more you will believe it. The more you believe that you can make a difference, the less tolerance you will have for what no longer works in our world. The more action you take, the more you inspire and empower others to do the same.

Once we shift our minds to accept that we are capable of doing something, we find a way to do it. Our planet is an ever-moving, ever-evolving place. The world has been telling us all that we are powerless and should live in fear—and *that* has been working. Now it is time for us to reprogram ourselves to awaken to our true power and purpose.

BEING A BEACON OF JOY

As I started to eventually find and live my purpose, I became *very* enthusiastic about it. When I realized that heaven actually did want me to have a happy life—and that when I allowed my heart to be open to it, the guidance to create my own happiness would come—I wanted everyone to know. I never had any intention to impose my beliefs upon anyone or preach my views without invitation—but I had friends at the time who I knew could benefit from angelic guidance because they had so many complaints about their own lives.

Anytime I was in a conversation about some part of their lives that wasn't going right, I knew I had a very helpful answer (*Ask the angels!*)—but I also had to respect their views, as they never expressed any enthusiasm for the spiritual lifestyle. We had other things in common, but spirituality didn't appear to be one of them.

I would never judge anyone for not thinking like me, but as you now know, when you work with angels to improve your life, the improvement doesn't eventually end or taper off—you're constantly working on yourself and constantly manifesting your next step in life. So when you spend time around those who complain about, but do not seem open to taking constructive steps toward improving, their lives—I can assure you with absolute certainty there will come a time when you have to ask yourself if these relationships are still serving you. This question will not come from selfishness or judgment—instead, you will feel the difference in your energy when you are around someone whose energy is stuck.

And you'll want to help, I'm sure—but how can you if they are not necessarily open to what you believe? And this is what my point is—those who strive for happiness often have trouble intermingling with those who refuse to believe in happiness.

Modeling spiritual connection is all heaven will ever really ask of us as far as influencing others to be open to asking for help. Whether those around you believe in, or even respect, who you are and what you believe, the differences in your life and energy will be undeniable. I can assure you that given enough time, people will become curious. They may even ask you questions about your life and faith.

Heaven does not ask us to impose our beliefs on others who are not open to hearing them—but the angels do want us to live our lives to the fullest, to allow nothing but higher energy into our presence so that we may serve as shining examples of the magnificence and authenticity of heavenly guidance. This is how heaven wants the truth of humanity's right to happiness to spread throughout our planet—through osmosis—in an organic way, where the clear benefits of living this sort of life are undeniably present.

It's the backbone to capitalism; but this same organic and sometimes subconscious spreading of desire is exactly how heaven wants to open up our planet to God's higher energy, and it is exactly why you should never feel guilty asking angels for help in your life.

It is time for us to live in harmony as a species, and the only way to accomplish that is to make sure every human on earth believes that true happiness is attainable. As I said before, the truth of God is that we are meant to be happy, and the more of us who open up to this fact (yes, I said *fact*), the easier it will be to live on this planet.

No longer will we compromise peace for security against threats that only exist because we are trying to *find* peace in nonpeaceful ways. No longer will the illusion that there is not enough happiness for all of us exist. No longer will we embrace the insanity that tells us fear and divisions are the only answer to our world's problems.

PRAYING IT FORWARD

In the Appendix, I'm going to introduce to you a few archangels that have not been discussed yet in this book so you have a chance to work with them if you feel guided. (The trio of archangels most helpful to call upon for working toward your life purpose—Nathaniel, Michael, and Raphael—were discussed in Part II.) Also in the Appendix, my wife, Peroshini, shares some sample prayers for you as a send-off on your life-purpose journey. Please use these prayers as a chance to introduce yourself to new energy and new vibrations and to see if there is an archangel that you especially resonate with.

So while these prayers will resonate differently with each person, I wanted to include them as a reminder that there literally are no limits to what we are allowed to pray for. Oftentimes we worry about asking for too much, but those are human impositions, and we should understand that heaven wants humanity to pray even more, not less. If more of us on this planet spent time praying confidently for what we want, we would spend substantially less time trying to find happiness by taking from others. God assures us that everything we need to live our purpose will be provided.

We humans are the ones that created the illusion that happiness is limited and hard to find. Even our monetary system is designed to reinforce this myth. Try this—look up the entire net worth of your country online; it's out there. Then take that number and divide it by the population of your country. That alone will tell you something.

It told me that in our current way of life, our society depends on a certain percentage of the people going without so that others may have abundance. Heaven wants to guide our planet into a new, more balanced and peaceful age of equality. Crime will abate because no one will be disadvantaged; wars will stop because we will find our happiness and peace from within through our discovery of purpose.

We have come a long way as a species: We have created a vast infrastructure that we take for granted. In most parts of the world, toilets flush, water runs, and lights turn on (and in the developing world many hardworking and generous souls are endeavoring to implement these conveniences). We have reached a developmental pinnacle as far as our earthly material needs are concerned, so it should never be seen as coincidence that now is the time heaven has chosen to wake us up to spiritual happiness and purpose.

Soon you will live in a world where we all revel in and take great pleasure in witnessing the happiness of others. When you talk to your angels every day, your motivations and desires will become aligned with the true and current needs of our planet. You can take heart knowing that not one person on our planet will be hungry or suffering needlessly.

Just imagine that for a second: So many of us enjoy the great feeling of being in a freshly cleaned house—let yourself feel for a second knowing that we have cleaned the planet of unnecessary suffering, inequality, and divisions. It's more possible than you think. Even the most "evil" people on this planet have deep desires for harmony—they are just confused as to what harmony actually is and how to get it.

The more of us that allow heaven's light, love, and guidance into our lives, the more visibility we will bring to the benefit of living this way, and the greater example we will be to others. The more people realize that the answer to so many of our questions lies in the simplicity of prayer and faith, the more this awakening will spread and the more peace we will know.

I completely understand that this may all seem idealistic—and I readily admit that it *is* idealistic. Part of my mission with this book has been, however, to convince you that *idealistic* does not mean "impossible," *dream* does not mean "fantasy," and large dreams are not more difficult to achieve than small ones. Who decided all of that in the first place? Let's wake up, stop perpetuating limiting thoughts, and understand that our existence on this planet can be whatever we want.

There are no scientific or universal laws that state that the best outcome has to be the least likely one. If we collectively want and believe in happiness, it *will* happen. How? It starts with you. Every single person who hands the weight of their worries and fears over to heaven and asks for guidance makes the world measurably lighter.

APPENDIX

Archangels of Manifestation

Ariel is the nature angel, with a feminine energy. This archangel oversees animals, birds, plants, and fairies. Call upon this archangel for emergency money, housing, and other earthly survival resources. Ariel helps with protection against severe weather; anything having to do with a home, be it finding a new one, leaving a bad one, or protecting the one you're in; or anything you need for your children, pets, or garden. Ariel is associated with lions and lionesses, so you can also call on her for courage and bravery.

Azrael is the angel of endings, death, and healing from grief. This can be in any aspect of life—jobs, relationships, and friendships. If you feel stuck, he can help to end these things and make sure you are guided during your transition period, as well as heal your heart so you can manifest new, higher-level situations. Archangel Azrael also eases losses so you get out of a negative pattern and don't hang on to anger, bitterness, and unforgiveness.

Chamuel's very name is about manifesting—it means "he who sees God." Chamuel is all-seeing, so he is what we call the *finding* angel. Having Chamuel's energy in your life is like hiring a life coach. He will help you to find not just a job, but the right job (or the right partner or house). He sees the truth underlying your wants and needs and helps you align your thoughts accordingly. If you have lost anything—objects, people, or memories—he is the archangel to call on.

Gabriel, the messenger of God, is very connected with manifesting pregnancies and anything having to do with childbirth, conception, or gestational health and well-being. This angel from the Bible's Book of Luke informed Mother Mary that she was pregnant with Jesus, famously saying, "Behold, I bring you good tidings of great joy." This messenger quality helps communicators such as speakers, writers, and teachers. Gabriel assists you in getting published or starting any direction in life having to do with communication, especially on a grand scale. Gabriel also helps with the arts—dancing, singing, acting, and so forth. With a "nudging" energy, this angel is sometimes a bit pushy. When you call on Gabriel, you *will* get pushed. Therefore, working with this powerful archangel is great for helping to get past procrastination.

Haniel's name means "grace of God." Very connected to mystical feminine energy and the full moon, she is a wonderful archangel to call upon for manifesting clairvoyance and psychic abilities and promoting general feminine health. In addition, she helps with situations that make you nervous, as she gives you grace.

Jeremiel is known as the angel that helps with the life review after death, but he can also help you with a life review *before* death. This amazing archangel often arrives on the scene at the times when you wake up and realize that you need direction. Jeremiel prompts you to ask, "What am I going to do with my life?" He also helps you recognize and get past situations that make you unhappy, and find more suitable replacements; let go of old anger, blame, and fear; and stop repeating the same patterns so you can move forward.

Jophiel is the archangel of beauty. She is skilled at helping you to manifest better energy in your house or your office/personal spaces. Jophiel brings more beauty into your life and surroundings and also helps you to afford beauty, such as art and crystals.

In addition, she helps you manifest whatever you need to make your life and surroundings more pleasing to you.

Metatron is the angel who helps highly sensitive young people (including Indigos) and those who are new to the spiritual path. He can help parents manifest more peace and order at home, including better behavior and healthier/stronger relationships within the family. He also assists with manifesting all aspects of spirituality, like finding your spiritual path and knowing what to educate yourself on and discerning what to potentially avoid.

Raguel is the "friendship" angel, the angel of harmonious relationships. Raguel assuages loneliness so we can find new, healthy friendships and relationships. He also helps us to create harmony in current ones. His name means "friend of God," so he oversees and guides us in all aspects of relationships.

Raziel is the angel of secrets and mysteries. He helps us to have a greater understanding of spiritual mysteries, break down the process of manifesting, and get in touch with divine timing. He also helps with karma and past-life blocks that come from vows of poverty and chastity. He helps to sever those vows and rid us of self-denial and self-punishment.

Sandalphon has a dual role as the angel who delivers prayers to heaven, and the angel of music and thus complete synchronization and mutual effort. Archangel Sandalphon assists with teamwork and ensuring everyone knows what to do and when. He helps musicians manifest good performances, along with the right themes, lyrics, and melodies in composition.

Uriel is the angel of light and wisdom. He helps students to manifest good grades, businesspeople to find good ideas, and all of us to know what is next on our path. Uriel is another amazing angel to work with to get rid of resentment and unforgiveness. He also helps us to release jealousy and unfavorable comparisons. This is the archangel to call upon to banish feelings of desperation and fears of not being successful.

Zadkiel is the memory angel, who helps you to remember everything you need along your path. When things get hectic, this angel will keep you grounded and collected. He is also a good angel to call upon during tests or in any situation where remembering specific information is important.

Manifestation Prayers by Peroshini Naidoo

My wife, Peroshini, has generously donated these prayers that she wrote specifically for this book. I want to reiterate and stress that there is absolutely no ritual and no rules necessary for prayer to be effective. Specificity and consistency are the keys to praying in a way that will attract the best possible life for you. Remember that although prayers are powerful, heaven is always listening to the needs and desires in your heart. So please maintain prayer as a regular part of your routine, but never forget that it is our responsibility to keep our minds clear of negative thinking, our hearts free of fear and hesitation, and our whole being open to whatever heaven brings us, as this is always the best possible outcome.

Prayer for Life Purpose

Dear Archangel Nathaniel, God, and all my guides and angels, please accompany me on my path. I give you full permission to intervene in my life for my highest good, in order for me to discover and live my true life purpose. I understand that my life choices are my own, but I do welcome your guidance in steering me in the direction of greatest happiness and soul growth. I wish to feel like I matter and that my life has a positive impact on this world. I know I have talents and gifts that can assist me and others on my path, and I call on you to help me uncover them.

All changes I must make will come easily and quickly, and I affirm that this will be an enjoyable process for me. I will rise above any initial fear and follow your guidance to my true life purpose. If at any time I encounter challenges, I will remain positive and keep faith that I will overcome all obstacles. I know that I may have placed limitations on myself regarding what I'm capable of, and I welcome your help, Archangel Nathaniel, in seeing past these blocks. Help me remain confident in myself and at peace throughout this process so I can enjoy the journey and live more in the moment. I'm ready for change and a new way of living that's more in sync with my dreams and goals. I deserve to discover and live my true life purpose, and I affirm my commitment to follow my guidance and take action toward realizing my dreams! Thank you, Archangel Nathaniel, God, and all my guides and angels, for your assistance.

Prayer to Help Raise Your Vibration

Dear angels, guides, and Creator, thank you for helping me raise my vibration so I attract only the best to and for me. Please assist me in letting go of all relationships that are unbalanced, harmful, or stagnant or which slow me down. I'm committed to releasing the habit of doing things out of obligation or because I feel guilty and want to be a good person. Guilt and obligation are lower-vibrating emotions, and I realize that they do not help me. Please guide me to release all situations that no longer serve a purpose in my life. The more old energy I release, the more room I will have for fresh, new energy.

I realize that in order to raise my vibration,
I must first show love and compassion toward
myself, and I welcome your help, angels, in doing
so. Though it's normal and okay to feel negative
at times, I commit to processing my emotions
and then releasing them to heaven so I can move
forward and attract the best possible situations to
me. Please help me clear all unhealthy and self-
destructive habits that are keeping me rooted in
lower-vibrational situations.

I know that I'm influenced by the energy
that I surround myself with, so please guide me,
angels, on how to bring high-vibrational activities
and people into my life. I want to be surrounded by
upbeat, positive people who will lift my mood and
help me maintain a happy outlook. I wish for my life
to be joyful, abundant, satisfying, and purposeful.
Please help me raise my vibration, angels,
so I attract this reality to me.

Prayer for Clear Intuition

Angels, Creator, and guides, please help
me to clearly hear, feel, and understand my
intuition. I know that you and my higher self speak
to me through this divine channel, and I wish to
strengthen this connection. Help me to rise above
any fear or lack of confidence that prevents me from
connecting with and recognizing my intuition. Help
me feel empowered and safe when my intuition
gives me a heads-up so that I am able to recognize
red flags and avoid people and situations that do
not serve my best interest. I know that my intuition
is a gift that is always available to me—help me to
access this blessing, angels, and to use it to
build a happier and more balanced life.

Prayer for Cord Cutting

Dear God and Archangel Michael, please help me
cut any cords I have to people and situations that
no longer serve a purpose in my life. Help me to
understand that I can move on without guilt or

sadness, as these feelings only hold me back. Please help me establish healthy energetic boundaries, Archangel Michael, so I don't allow the opinions and feelings of others to "camp out" in my energy field.

I'm ready for positive change, and I know that the energy of the past has no place in my present life. I wish to not only cut my cords but also to learn how to empower myself so that I'm more in control of my own energy. In truth, I know that when I fully commit to moving on and accepting that the only power people and situations hold over me is what I allow, I will be free from lower energy and ready for a new beginning.

Prayer for Forgiveness

Dear Creator and Archangel Chamuel, please help me channel your healing light and release all stagnant, lower energy from my soul. I now let go of resentment, anger, jealousy, sadness, regret, and all other emotions that keep me stuck in the past. I wish to move on with my life and forgive those who have hurt me. I realize that any emotional damage I

have suffered cannot ruin my life
if I'm willing to heal and move on.

Help me remember that I'm perfect as I am and
strong enough to rise above any pain or trauma
that I've encountered. With your help, I can release
all disappointment in others and remember that I
am here for a higher purpose. Help me to see the
bigger picture and have faith that there is a reason
for everything, Archangel Chamuel. Help me see the
good in every situation and every person. From this
day forward, I aim to forgive and be a source of light
and love to all I encounter on my path.

Prayer for Healthy Relationships

God and Archangel Jophiel, please help me to
love myself and remember all the things that are
wonderful about me even when others do not.
Help me establish healthy boundaries so I do not
overextend myself or ignore my own needs.
Help me to take the time to nurture my inner
child and acknowledge any feelings of not being
appreciated or loved that I may secretly harbor.

I wish to be guided away from critical, judgmental
people who drain my energy and dampen my
mood. I'm ready for equal relationships, where
the energy and attention I freely share is returned.
Please help me surround myself with balanced
relationships based on mutual love and
respect, for my highest good.

Prayer for a New Career

Thank you, God and angels, for helping
me find a new career that brings me joy and
satisfaction. I'm grateful that I am able to utilize
my unique skills and gifts in this new profession.
I'm happy that my needs are met and that I'm
financially abundant. Thank you for remaining
with me and guiding me while I embark on this
new phase of life. I'm grateful for this wonderful
blessing and overjoyed at how divinely everything
has worked out for everyone involved. My happiness
and success are a gift I share with the world! I love
my new career. Thank you again, God and
angels, for helping guide me to it.

Appendix

Prayer for Past-Life Healing

God and Archangel Nathaniel, please remain with me and help me heal from all past-life experiences that are not aligned with my soul purpose in this lifetime. Please work with me and clear me of all blocks, trauma, and fear carried over from other lifetimes so I can stay focused on my path and be of service to heaven. Help me remember anything from other lifetimes that may be keeping me from my full potential and help me to understand that there is no need to hold on to this old energy.

I know that my soul is limitless and cannot be damaged unless I choose a reality where this is possible. In truth, I'm meant to be happy, and nothing from a past life can hold me back. Thank you, Archangel Nathaniel, for helping me stay focused on these truths. I'm grateful for your intervention and affirm my commitment to live a life filled with joy, purpose, and love.

Prayer for Perfect Health

Thank you, God and Archangel Raphael, for clearing my energy and helping me achieve a reality where I am healthy and happy. I'm ready for a new life and welcome any and all positive change. Guide me as to how I can incorporate healthier practices into my daily life, and help me find the strength to release all harmful habits. I take responsibility for my own well-being and ask that you please guide me on ways to strengthen my body both physically and energetically.

I'm ready for a new beginning and the reality I've always dreamed of—one where I'm able to be a full participant in life and do all the things I've wished for. Thank you for working with me, Archangel Raphael, and for keeping my thoughts focused on perfect health, today and always.

Prayer for Relief from Stress

Creator, please send Your angels to surround me and help me through this stressful time. With Your assistance, I can remain calm and centered inside even though my circumstances are challenging.

Angels, please cut any cords I have to lower energy, especially the energy of fear, drama, and chaos. Help me raise my vibration and disconnect from all stress, for my highest good. Help me stay positive and optimistic, and guide me to make any needed changes to my life. I'm tired of being overwhelmed and worried and gratefully hand this problem over to you. I know that this difficult time is only temporary, and with your help my reality will once again be one of peace and happiness. Thank you, Creator and my angels and guides, for your assistance.

ABOUT THE AUTHOR

Charles Virtue is the eldest son of Doreen Virtue—creator of the Angel Therapy Practitioner® (ATP) course and author of numerous books on working with angels. In touch with the angels and their guidance since childhood, Charles took profound interest in his mother's ATP classes, collaborating on them from their conception. For over seven years, he worked alongside Doreen, observing firsthand the power of the angels and their loving guidance.

As a certified ATP, Charles began to give readings with angel oracle cards in his early twenties, helping people learn how to clear the blocks and fears that kept them from hearing the true guidance that their angels wanted them to receive. His own connection with the angels guided him to share the gifts they bring to our lives.

At that point, his mission was clear: He wanted to teach people how to manifest, move toward, and live their life purpose by listening to their angels and inner guidance. Since 2007, he has helped thousands of people in over 24 countries to connect with a higher energy. Charles's down-to-earth teaching style aims to demonstrate that spirituality brings real-world blessings. Having witnessed countless people awaken to their guidance and purpose in his classes, he maintains the motto "Yes, it really is that easy."

Highly experienced in the field of manifestation, Charles combines his natural intuition with the knowledge obtained through a lifetime of exposure to the metaphysical world to offer his Angel Certification Program (ACP), Mediumship, Life Purpose/Manifestation, and Teacher Training classes. Most are available as home-study courses, in convenient downloadable formats. In addition, he is the co-author (with Doreen Virtue) of the books *Signs from Above* and *Awaken Your Indigo Power*, along with the *Indigo Angel Oracle Cards*, which are available at www.hayhouse.com and most major book retailers.

Website: www.CharlesVirtue.com

Hay House Titles of Related Interest

We hope you enjoyed this Hay House book. If you'd like to receive our online catalog featuring additional information on Hay House books and products, or if you'd like to find out more about the Hay Foundation, please contact:

Hay House, Inc., P.O. Box 5100, Carlsbad, CA 92018-5100
(760) 431-7695 or (800) 654-5126
(760) 431-6948 (fax) or (800) 650-5115 (fax)
www.hayhouse.com® • www.hayfoundation.org

———

Published in Australia by: Hay House Australia Pty. Ltd.,
18/36 Ralph St., Alexandria NSW 2015
Phone: 612-9669-4299 • *Fax:* 612-9669-4144
www.hayhouse.com.au

Published in the United Kingdom by: Hay House UK, Ltd.,
The Sixth Floor, Watson House, 54 Baker Street, London W1U 7BU
Phone: +44 (0)20 3927 7290 • *Fax:* +44 (0)20 3927 7291
www.hayhouse.co.uk

Published in India by: Hay House Publishers India,
Muskaan Complex, Plot No. 3, B-2, Vasant Kunj, New Delhi 110 070
Phone: 91-11-4176-1620 • *Fax:* 91-11-4176-1630
www.hayhouse.co.in

———

Access New Knowledge.
Anytime. Anywhere.

Learn and evolve at your own pace
with the world's leading experts.

www.hayhouseU.com

Printed in the United States
by Baker & Taylor Publisher Services